MOSAIC RENAISSANCE

Reviving Classic Tile Art With Millefiori

Laurel Skye

NORTH LIGHT BOOKS

North Light Books
Cincinnati, Ohio
www.mycraftivity.com

MOSAIC RENAISSANCE. Copyright © 2009 by Laurel Skye. Manufactured in China. All rights reserved. The patterns and drawings in the book are for personal use of reader. By permission of the author and publisher, they may be either hand-traced or photocopied to make single copies, but under no circumstances may they be resold or republished. It is permissible for the purchaser to make the projects contained herein and sell them at fairs, bazaars and craft shows. No other part of this book may be reproduced in any form or by any electronic or mechanical means including information storage and retrieval systems without permission in writing from the publisher, except by a reviewer, who may quote a brief passage in review. Published by North Light Books, an imprint of F+W Media, Inc., 4700 East Galbraith Road, Cincinnati, Ohio 45236. (800) 289-0963. First edition.

13 12 11 10 09   5 4 3 2 1

Distributed in Canada by Fraser Direct
100 Armstrong Avenue
Georgetown, ON, Canada L7G 5S4
Tel: (905) 877-4411

Distributed in the U.K. and Europe by David & Charles
Brunel House, Newton Abbot, Devon, TQ12 4PU, England
Tel: (+44) 1626 323200, Fax: (+44) 1626 323319
E-mail: postmaster@davidandcharles.co.uk

Distributed in Australia by Capricorn Link
P.O. Box 704, S. Windsor, NSW 2756 Australia
Tel: (02) 4577-3555

Library of Congress Cataloging-in-Publication Data
Skye, Laurel.
  Mosaic renaissance / Laurel Skye. -- 1st ed.
      p. cm.
  Includes bibliographical references and index.
  ISBN 978-1-60061-198-8 (pbk. : alk. paper)
  1. Mosaics--Technique. 2. Handicraft. I. Title.
  TT910.S57 2009
  738.5--dc22
                                    2009014089

Editor: Kristin Boys
Designer: Steven Peters
Production Coordinator: Greg Nock
Photographers: Adam Hand, Ric Deliantoni,
            Christine Polomsky
Photo Stylist: Jan Nickum

www.fwmedia.com

METRIC CONVERSION CHART

to convert	to	multiply by
Inches	Centimeters	2.54
Centimeters	Inches	0.4
Feet	Centimeters	30.5
Centimeters	Feet	0.03
Yards	Meters	0.9
Meters	Yards	1.1
Sq. Inches	Sq. Centimeters	6.45
Sq. Centimeters	Sq. Inches	0.16
Sq. Feet	Sq. Meters	0.09
Sq. Meters	Sq. Feet	10.8
Sq. Yards	Sq. Meters	0.8
Sq. Meters	Sq. Yards	1.2
Pounds	Kilograms	0.45
Kilograms	Pounds	2.2
Ounces	Grams	28.3
Grams	Ounces	0.035

Dedication

To Brian Sproul, a visionary artist whom few knew. For twenty-five years, he created art unceasingly from his wheelchair and through his pain. He died unknown. And Robert, eighty-six, an ex-marine, alcoholic widower, who turned his house and yards into a mosaic wonderland and grotto, only to see it vandalized again and again by neighborhood kids. He is an unsung hero. To all those brilliant visionaries who are broken and damaged and still create out of their fractured realms. I applaud you for not quitting and for your courage to continue to make art.

Acknowledgments
The Quantum Physics of Writing a Book

Nothing exists inherently on its own. Everything is interconnected to everything else. Example: a tree. A tree would not exist if not for three factors:

1. The connection to its whole and its parts (roots, trunk, branches, leaves)
2. Its relation to its environment (earth, rain, air, wind, sun)
3. How it is observed (the viewers' perception of it)

So how does this book exist?

The Whole and Its Parts: My vision (the roots), talking about it and endless rewriting (the truck), connecting with Tonia Davenport, Kristin Boys, Christine Polomsky and all the good people at North Light Books (the limbs and the leaves), and their ability to act on what was just an idea.

The Environment: My extended family and friends with their tireless support. To Zo Devine, my Italian friends Julia and Daniela for when I was lost in translation. To my sons, whom I adore: Serge (who taught me computer skills) and Jesh (who taught me courage). And especially to my daughter, Kiah who helped to write and create this mosaic book with me. Lastly, to my ex-husband, Dov, for had he not left me, this mosaic journey and this book would never have happened.

The Observer: You! The reader that observes this effort in your own unique way and then takes the "mosaic ball" and runs with it.

So I acknowledge the beautifully orchestrated universal workings that we are all a part of, that made this book and all creative journeys possible.

Contents

Introduction: *Reinventing Shangri-la*

It all started in 1955 when I was nine years old. I was glued to the black-and-white television screen. There was Charlie Chan in Paris, with its sensual Parisian Apache dance, the lavishness of Brazilian bombshell Carmen Miranda, with all the seductive exoticism of South America, Mr. Moto in Shanghai and James Hilton's idea of Shangri-la in the 1937 movie, *Lost Horizons*. I was hooked on the exotic turbaned fortune-tellers, carnivals and séances. I wanted to conjure a phantasmagorical world— spiritual, beyond reality, elaborate and mysterious, mystical, magical, oriental and flamboyant.

At fourteen, I ran away to join the circus. No, not really. But I did move to Hollywood and sang in coffee houses. I wanted to be a set designer, write music and make costumes. A seed in my childhood had been planted, which would keep alive the lure of mysterious, faraway places like Tibet's gilded temples and monasteries, embroidered silks, yak butter tea, rich intricate paintings, and ornate Mongolian carvings.

So, how did I work all that into a nine-to-five job? Well, I didn't. Instead I hung out with West African musicians and made music. I also made clothes, hats, jewelry, greeting cards, calendars, leather belts and bags. I even made chopsticks and crochet needles. I traveled, slept on the side of the road, ate ceremonial peyote with Native elders in New Mexico, lived in communes, hung out with people as diverse as Frank Zappa and Charles Bukowski. I opened a small restaurant and juiced exotic drinks and elixirs and served dishes as foreign as forbidden rice. I knitted, crocheted, sewed, raised goats, spun yarn and made cheese. And, oh yes, I tiled things.

One thing led to another and the next thing I knew, I turned fifty. There I was, three marriages and four children later. With fifty, came caring for my aging mother, who died blissfully in my arms. A twenty-two year marriage culminated in separation. With divorce came a lack of money. And with turning fifty, there came raging hormones, depression and hot flashes. And my dog died. That year I thought I would die, too.

That was the year I had to choose to throw in the towel or get back on the train. I got back on. I picked up tiling again. It saved me. I traveled, I studied, I grew, and day after day I didn't die. It was during this period that I decided to go to Italy and study mosaics from the masters. While in Ravenna, I explored, in awe, the Basilica of St. Vitale with a group of like-minded mosaicists. But, always the loner, I found myself turning left when everyone else was turning right, splintering off from the group. It was in my meandering that I stumbled across what was to be the next chapter in my life's journey: the work of Dusciana Bravura and her father, Marco. I was mesmerized. Dusciana had taken millefiori slices and used them as tiles. Never before had I seen any mosaics like it. I had an epiphany, if you will. From that day on, I knew what I wanted to do.

I've never lost my fascination with the depth of pattern, color and richness of millefiori. Couple millefiori with the extraordinary wealth of glass and tiles the world has to offer and there are endless possibilities for weaving mosaic tapestries. As you follow the work throughout this book, I hope you will feel the unity of the fabric of the world: African, Middle Eastern, European, Asian, Spanish and Tibetan. They are here, all elements woven into and through the mosaics of my childhood dreams and middle-age reality, in harmony and fusion. They are all *vetro tessuto*—weavings of tapestry in glass!

Tesserae, Tools and Techniques

BASIC INFORMATION AND TECHNIQUES FOR GETTING STARTED

Let's talk about starting a project. I like to start by procrastinating. Really. Before I begin, I need to dream or percolate a project into being. There is a lot that can be achieved during that time of not doing anything. That percolating allows you the passive productive time for your vision to form. This is the time when your art starts to express your mood and your personality. This is the start of "it" becoming "you."

This is not a cerebral process, it's a visionary one. Too much thinking and you get "analysis paralysis" and never get anything started. Release some of your need to control the outcome and give yourself permission to make mistakes as you take chances, leaps of faith, change your mind and allow for that element of spontaneous creation to take place. It is often in this junction where the magic happens. Give yourself permission to procrastinate, percolate and dream. It's all part of the creative process.

And it's all about you, the creator. You are the conduit through which the ever-abundant river of creative juices flows. As you open to that source and direct it to your mosaic projects, you start your journey. So the first, and primary, tool is you!

Now, let's gather some other tools, and head for that magical junction where time and timelessness intersect—where you stop tracking time and start the creative process! I have laid out a few of the most useful tools and materials I use on a regular basis. You'll also learn the essentials for basic mosaic techniques such as priming, grouting and cutting.

Essential Tools and Materials

If you were going to build a house what would you need? Some lumber, a saw, hammer and nails, right? In the same way, when you are creating a mosaic you need a basic set of tools and materials on hand, namely tiles, cutters and glue.

Tesserae

Tessera is the term for any singular tile within a mosaic. *Tesserae* is plural, and most commonly used to refer to all your mosaic tiles. The types I use most often for the projects in the book are:

VITREOUS GLASS: These glass mosaic tiles, made in molds from a glass paste, usually come in ¾" (2cm) squares. The top side is smooth while the underside is ridged for better adhesion.

CERAMIC: Mini ceramics are great for using with glass because they are thinner than regular ceramic, and so are comparable to glass in height.

SMALTI: These are small rectangular pieces of opaque and/or transparent glass produced in Italy and Mexico. I use all colors, but I especially like 24-karat gold and gold colorati.

STAINED GLASS: I use both sheets and precut shapes (most often available in ½" [13mm] and ¾" [2cm]).

VAN GOGH GLASS: Not a traditional stained glass, these glass tiles have a fern pattern that is accentuated by metallic paints fused onto the back, making a unique addition to a mosaic piece.

For the projects in the book, and for tiling with millefiori in general, you can use whatever colors and types of tile your heart desires! In fact, the materials lists in chapter 3 do not include specific colors or tiles for this reason. Don't be reluctant to use your "good stuff." My mother used to say, "You can't make good coffee unless you start out with good coffee beans!" That said, some of my favorite types of tesserae are pictured below.

1. transparent smalti
2. iridium
3. smalti
4. smalto
5. cathedral glass
6. ice jade iridescent
7. dichroic glass
8. glitter glass
9. mirror glass
10. stained glass
11. vitreous glass
12. van Gogh glass
13. papau shell
14. tapestry glass
15. metallic van Gogh glass

Millefiori

Millefiori is formed in the hot furnaces on the picturesque island of Murano, just outside of Venice, Italy. Although millefiori has been around for centuries, I believe one of its earliest appearances in mosaic artwork goes back to Maestro Felice Nittolo in the 1970s. It wasn't until the early 1990s, mainly through the work of the Bravura family, that millefiori rose to its present place in the global mosaic limelight. Often called eye candy for good reason, *millefiori* literally translates into "one thousand flowers," and offers colorful, immediate patterning to add to mosaic designs.

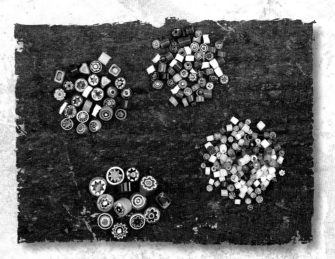

HOW MILLEFIORI IS MADE

While molten hot, glass is stretched into extraordinarily long, thin rods, called cane. Most often available by the ounce or gram, millefiori is sold in precut slices, revealing the cross section of pattern within. These pieces can then be used whole or halved in mosaic patterns.

SIZES OF MILLEFIORI

Millefiori comes in a variety of sizes, starting as small as 2–3mm and going up to 12–14mm. For most of the projects in this book, you will use 5–6mm to 8–10mm.

VARYING THICKNESSES

Cutting of the cane makes for varying thicknesses in millefiori pieces. Very thin slices are great for setting just slightly into the surface of the mastic. Thicker cuts help your dollar go further, since they can be cut into quarters.

CONCAVE AND CONVEX

When setting millefiori, notice if there is a concave or convex side. It is best to set the concave side face down into the bedding of mastic and the convex side face up to keep the piece secure. Always bury any sharp edges in the mastic.

TRANSPARENT AND OPAQUE

Millefiori is made either transparent or opaque. If you're tiling over glass and want the light to show through (such as on a candleholder), choose transparent millefiori. Both types work well over opaque surfaces.

Cutting Tools

What tools are crucial for doing mosaic? Well, for the minimalist, tiles and a rock to smash them with would probably do. For everyone else wanting a little more precision and control, here is a short list of essentials (from left to right in photo):

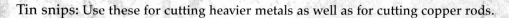

Wire cutters: These are best for cutting lightweight metal such as copper wire and ball chain.

Running pliers: Angled for leverage, use these pliers to snap scored stained glass with a light squeeze. Most stained glass suppliers offer running pliers, and any brand will do.

Tile nippers: Also called side-biters, these are good for cutting most ceramic tiles and dishes. Several brands of nippers are available anywhere tiles are sold.

Wheeled glass cutters: This tool is great for cutting all your glass tesserae. Several brands of glass cutters are available online from mosaic suppliers. I suggest QEP cutters because they have a great spring action and are easy on joints.

Tin snips: Use these for cutting heavier metals as well as for cutting copper rods.

Pistol grip (bottom row): This tool is filled with cutting oil to facilitate easy scoring of stained glass pieces. I recommend the Toyo pistol grip and Toyo cutting oil.

Adhesive

It's best to keep a posse of adhesives in your mosaic laboratory to meet the challenges of adhering different types of tiles and materials to various surfaces. Here are some essential adhesives:

Mastic: This works well when you need an adhesive that is easy to spread with a quick grab. You will use mastic for most of the projects in chapter 3, as it works well for adhering tile. Mapei Type 1 is my first choice for mastic because it blends well with color additives without losing its tackiness. (See page 14 for more on tinting mastic.)

Silicone: This adheres well to glass and dries clear. Keep in mind that silicone usually has a short working time, and there is a short window of opportunity for cleaning up glue from unwanted spaces. Most silicone adhesives will work for the projects in this book, but I like Silicone II because it spreads well and has a longer working time than most.

PVA (white) glue: My glue of choice is MAC glue (but I also use Weldbond frequently). MAC glue is a nontoxic liquid adhesive that dries clear and works well for adhering glass to glass.

Epoxy: Magic Smooth epoxy is an easy-to-use two-part epoxy that is water soluble and without fumes, plus it has a long working time (60–90 minutes). I use it for adhering difficult materials (like glass to metal) and on projects that will be exposed to elements. Douglas and Sturgess (resin #7828 and hardener #8140) is easy to spread and works great for affixing tempered glass over paper.

Grouting Materials

Gather these special materials for grouting all your projects. See more about grouting on page 16.

Dry grout: Used as the base for mixing wet grout for projects. It also works to remove excess wet grout during grouting. I use sanded grout almost exclusively.

Grouting elf: This is a useful tool for getting into tight spaces, packing air pockets and removing excess grout.

Sponge: You'll want a professional-quality sponge with finer holes. This works best for packing grout into air pockets. And they won't shred. Cut large sponges into sections for easier handling.

Miscellaneous Tools and Materials

You can find things around the house for working on mosaics, and the few below may also be found at your local hardware store (or pet store!). Others will come in handy, but these are the essentials:

Acrylic paint: Golden is my favorite line of paints for its broad spectrum of colors and ability to stick to difficult surfaces.

Copper foil tape: Use this self-adhesive tape to finish rough wooden edges and for soldering. Copper tape is sold in most stained glass supply stores in a variety of thicknesses and widths.

Craft knife: This is a must-have for cleaning adhesive that has dried on the surface of tiles.

Hammer: Use for shattering tempered glass sheets, adding hooks to trivets and mirrors.

Hollow copper tubing and wire: Wrapping 22-gauge wire around the tubing makes for unique embellishments that embed well into mastic.

Metal palette knife: Great for spreading mastic evenly (and better than a plastic palette knife).

Paintbrushes: Keep plenty of sizes on hand for various paint applications. Disposable sponge brushes are good for applying primers, which don't require precise application.

Sculpting epoxy: Magic Sculp epoxy (my favorite) is a water-soluble, two-part sculpting material that dries to a rock-hard surface. Use it for sculpting faux found objects and tiling soft items like shoes.

Tongue depressor, craft stick or plastic palette knife: These are all disposable so they're great for mixing and spreading gooey adhesives.

Tweezers: Long tweezers are essential for handling small tesserae and millefiori.

Veterinary syringe: Use this handy tool for directing mastic into hard-to-reach spaces.

For more essential tools and materials see Tinting Mastic (page 14), Priming (page 15)
and Working With Grout (page 16).

Working With Mastic

You'll need mastic on hand for most mosaic projects; mastic works to adhere tile to surfaces.

Tinting Mastic

Colored mastic adheres as well as white mastic, so tinting it is simply a matter of personal preference. I always tint mastic when tiling with millefiori. When a project is left ungrouted, the mastic will show between the tiles, so I tint the mastic a color that complements the tesserae. I prefer dark gray, but you can choose any color you like. Even when grouting, I tint, just in case mastic shows through the grout.

For tinting, I use mostly powdered, concentrated pigments ground from oxides and minerals and made for use with grout. Diamond Tech International produces quality powdered pigments, and Tints-All makes good pigments that come in tubes.

1. ADD PIGMENT TO MASTIC

Since it is concentrated, a little bit of pigment goes a long way, so start with a small amount of it. Mix the powder into the mastic.

2. MIX PIGMENT

As you mix, check for dry pockets of powder, especially at the bottom. Stir until the color becomes a shade lighter than the desired color. If it is still too light, add a bit more color. Be careful: Too much powder may compromise the adhesive nature.

3. FINISH MIXING

Continue mixing until all the powder has been blended and you achieve your desired color. Cover it securely with a tight fitting lid. This mixture can be kept for months.

WHAT YOU'LL NEED:

container for mastic
pigment
white mastic
plastic knife

Troubleshooting: Dried-out mastic

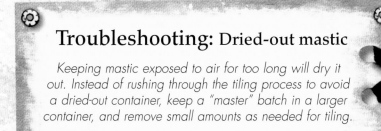

Keeping mastic exposed to air for too long will dry it out. Instead of rushing through the tiling process to avoid a dried-out container, keep a "master" batch in a larger container, and remove small amounts as needed for tiling.

Spreading Mastic

When setting millefiori in a bed of mastic, it's okay to have a case of the Goldilocks—the need to get things just right. If you spread a layer too thin, your millefiori could pop off. Too thick and you'll bury them in depths unseen.

THIS ONE IS TOO THIN ...
This slice of millefiori is simply "glued" to the surface, with the mastic only touching the bottom of the piece. There is no depth to the adhesive bedding.

THIS ONE IS TOO THICK ...
A bedding that is too thick will drown your pieces (and make a huge mess as all that mastic comes oozing out). You don't want to hide your millefiori in a mass of mastic.

THIS ONE IS JUST RIGHT!
The mastic bedding should be about one-third the height of your thickest millefiori. This will give you enough depth to sink larger or more irregular pieces deep while thinner ones will rest nearer to the surface

How Much Mastic Is Enough?

When you set tile in a layer of mastic, you should feel a connection between the tile and mastic. But if the mastic oozes up so high that it rises flush with the surface of the millefiori slice, you are using too much. Also, don't push your tiles down to the base of your work; just set them gently into the mastic.

Priming

Most surfaces you work with will require priming before you do anything else.

WHAT YOU'LL NEED:
Priming Kit
sandpaper (40 grit)
mosaic primer (like Mosaic Mercantile)
brush

1. SAND AND SCORE
If you have a finished surface (like a light switch plate), sand off the finish using sandpaper. Next, give it tooth by folding the sandpaper and scoring the surface with the folded edge, creating hatch marks.

2. SEAL
Dust off the surface to remove debris. Brush the primer over the surface. Doing so will close off the porosity of a surface such as wood. Sealing also helps the adhesive lock on to a surface.

Working With Grout

Grouting can be fun. It can be messy, too. The process of grouting is reminiscent of making mud pies in kindergarten. Grouting helps stabilize a mosaic and also provides a background to accent your design.

Mixing Grout

Grouting will always be the last step of a project (well, right before admiring your work!). You'll need to whip up a batch of grout before you actually start to do the dirty work.

WHAT YOU'LL NEED:

bowl

dry grout (I use charcoal colored most of the time)

sponge

water

latex gloves or plastic knife

1. ADD WATER

Start by squeezing a wet sponge over the dry grout, adding a bit of water at a time. (This gives you control over the amount of water added.)

2. MIX

Using a gloved hand, mix the grout with the water, with the objective of making a consistency of peanut butter or a brownie mix. I know some people are grossed out by putting their hands into this mix, so if you would rather use a disposable putty knife, that's fine.

Troubleshooting: Grout that's too thin

When starting out, many people don't add enough water and get grout that's too dry. They overcompensate by placing the container of grout under the tap and running too much water into it. The result is a mixture like miso soup. So, to avoid too-thin grout, stay away from the tap!

Appying Grout

Now it's time for the fun part!

WHAT YOU'LL NEED:

Grouting Kit

wet grout	dry grout
latex gloves	sponge
grouting elf	

1. WORK GROUT INTO SPACES

Drop a lump of grout onto the mosaic piece. Wearing gloves, massage the grout into the spaces between the tiles.

2. PULL OFF EXCESS GROUT

Use your fingers to feel for unfilled spaces. Pack in more grout as needed, working over uneven tile areas carefully. After the piece is covered, use your finger or grouting elf to pull off the excess grout.

3. COVER WITH DRY GROUT

While grout is still wet, cover the wet grout with a pile of dry grout. Rub the dry grout into the wet grout with firm pressure in a circular motion using your fingertips. The dry grout helps eliminate air pockets you may have missed. The abrasion also removes excess grout, shortening messy sponging time.

4. BUFF OFF GROUT MIX

Buff off the bulk of the wet/dry grout, then continue cleaning off clumped grout residue with the grout elf.

5. SPONGE OFF GROUT

Wet a sponge and wring out the excess water before swiping it across the surface to remove any remaining grout. Rotate your sponge to a clean side each time you wipe.

Finishing Touches

To make for a grout job that is picture perfect, follow these tips:

- Wipe one section with the sponge only once or twice at a time. Repeatedly sponging over the same area will remove grout from the spaces and spread a layer of film over the surface.
- When the piece is almost done, dry it carefully with a soft cloth.
- Check your dried mosaic to see where some "excavation" might be necessary. Use a craft knife to clean unwanted grout off the surface of the tiles.
- After about 72 hours, clean your piece with white vinegar, buffing the surface to a beautiful shine.

Cutting Techniques

When you cut your tesserae you will open a door to more pattern-making options because you can create all sorts of shapes and sizes. The holding methods that I suggest for cutting may be a bit awkward at first, but stay with it because these techniques will help you achieve a secure hold on your tile for cleaner, more exact cuts. Plus, you'll have fewer pieces flying away and hitting the floor, leaving you wondering "where in the %*$# did that go!"

Description of Cuts

Here you can see different cuts you can make from whole pieces of tile and millefiori. You'll want to refer to these descriptions when cutting tesserae for the projects in chapter 3.

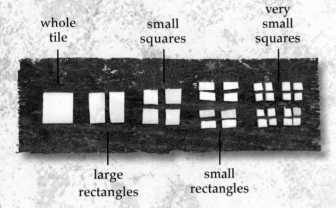

whole tile · small squares · very small squares · large rectangles · small rectangles

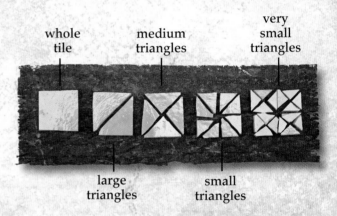

whole tile · medium triangles · very small triangles · large triangles · small triangles

SQUARES AND RECTANGLES

These pieces show different sizes cut from one ¾" (2cm) tile using the Point, Pinch, Pop method (page 20).

TRIANGLES

These pieces show different sizes cut from one ¾" (2cm) tile using the Point, Pinch, Pop method (page 20).

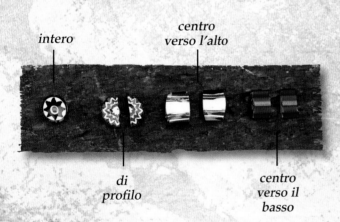

intero · centro verso l'alto · di profilo · centro verso il basso

thin rectangle · outlines

MILLEFIORI IN FOUR WAYS

These pieces show different ways to use cut millefiori (page 19).
intero: whole slices
di profilo: cut in half, cross section face up
centro verso l'alto: cut in half, cut side up
centro verso il basso: cut in half, cut side down

THIN RECTANGLES

These pieces show two ways to use rectangles cut from one ¾" (2cm) tile using the Tunnel Hold method (page 22).
thin rectangles: set flat side down
outlines: set cut side down

Cutting Millefiori

Even though each whole millefiori is a design in itself, it can be manipulated to form different shapes for creating more patterns. Cutting millefiori makes your tile go further, as well as offering different ways to achieve a rich pattern or texture in one's mosaic.

WHAT YOU'LL NEED:

millefiori
wheeled glass cutters

CUT IN HALF

The easiest and most reliable way to cut millefiori is right through the center of the pattern. Hold the outer sides with your thumb and index finger while cutting.

CUT IN HALF QUARTERS

The halves of thick pieces can be cut again through the belly, giving you four quarter sections from one whole millefiori.

WRONG WAY TO CUT

When cutting a whole piece of millefiori, this is the most difficult way to cut it in half. Cutting the glass from the side, through the "skin," will usually result in slivers ... and frustration.

SAVE A JAGGED PIECE

Have a crooked cut? No problem! Use your wheeled cutters like scissors and just trim away the jagged edge.

CREATE ROSETTES

Plant a mosaic garden in a heartbeat! Set a whole piece of millefiori first (*intero*). Then place four half-cuts (*di profilo*) around the whole piece.

Point, Pinch, Pop Method

I devised this holding method to be used with wheeled glass cutters while working with different types of glass tiles (i.e., stained glass, vitreous glass and smalti). This hold will give you excellent control over your glass, as your thumb will naturally be in alignment with your proposed cut line and lay next to your wheel, acting as a guide. This cutting method is especially useful for cutting on the diagonal, achieving uniform triangles.

WHAT YOU'LL NEE

glass tiles
wheeled glass cutters

1. POINT

Point your index finger while the thumb and middle finger pinch the tile. If you're right-handed, do this with your left hand. Your right hand will hold the cutters.

2. PINCH

Pinch the left side of the tile, against the flat surface, with your thumb and middle finger. Your thumb should align with the proposed cut line (represented in the photo by the dotted line). Pinch the other side of the tile, along the edge, with your index finger.

3. POP

Place the wheeled cutters over the center of the tile, over the cut line. Now pop your tile in half!

⚙ The Fourth P ⚙

It's helpful to add a fourth P—pray—right before you pop. This moment of prayer is not so much, "Oh, heavenly Father help me to make a good cut." It's more like taking a moment to line up your intended cut, breathing, planning on making a straight cut, then aiming and … pop!

CUT A RECTANGLE IN HALF

Use the Point, Pinch, Pop method to cut your rectangular piece into two smaller squares.

CUT A TRIANGLE

Use the Point, Pinch, Pop method to cut triangles. However, make your cut along the diagonal and place your index finger on the corner.

CUT CURVES

Using the Point, Pinch, Pop method results in straight cuts. But sometimes you want a curved piece. Cutting rectangles from the edge of the tile instead of down the center will give you a curved cut.

CUT SMALTI

You can cut smalti using wheeled cutters and the Point, Pinch, Pop method. (The color is most brilliant with the cut side facing up.) Cutting too close to the edge of the glass results in curved cuts, so be careful to cut in the center.

CUT SMALL CERAMIC TILES

Cutting small ceramic tiles using tile nippers is slightly different than the Point, Pinch, Pop method. Pinch the tile with your index and middle fingers behind the tile and the thumb in front, at the base of the tile and partly over the cut line. Place nippers about $\frac{1}{8}$" (3mm) into the tile. Now pop! These halves can also be cut in half again.

Troubleshooting: Dull blades

To avoid dulling blades, it's important to use the right tool for the job. Cutting ceramic with wheeled glass cutters will dull your blades very quickly. Be sure to cut ceramic with tile nippers.

Tunnel Hold Method

I use this cutting method to create four thin rectangles from one glass tile. (Using this method, as opposed to the Point, Pinch, Pop method results in more consistency in size among the rectangles.)

WHAT YOU'LL NEED:

glass tiles
wheeled glass cutters

1. HOLD TILE
Place your middle finger to the left of the proposed cut line and the index finger to the right (both at the top). With your thumb, support the base of the cut line on the bottom.

2. CUT WHOLE TILE
Place the wheeled cutters in the center and hold firmly, making a quick pop to cut the tile in half.

3. CUT HALVES
Now cut each half. Support the half firmly with your index finger on top and thumb below. Center the cutters in the middle of the rectangle, hold securely and make a very fast pop.

Outlines

The widths of thin rectangles cut with the Tunnel Hold method, no matter how careful you are, will always vary, and they will have slightly jagged edges. When you want to have a thin, continuous line with an even width in a mosaic pattern, use what I call outlines.

WHAT YOU'LL NEED:

glass tiles
wheeled glass cutters

SET OUTLINES
First, cut thin rectangles using the Tunnel Hold method. Instead of setting these cut rectangles in the mosaic as you normally would—with the cut edges facing side to side (see rectangles on the left)—set them with the cut edges facing up (see rectangles on the right). The outlines will appear more consistent in size because their widths are all the thickness of the tile.

Cutting Stained Glass

For projects with a contemporary look or when you need specific shapes for creating patterns, you can cut pieces from stained glass sheets using a pistol grip.

WHAT YOU'LL NEED:

sheets of stained glass
pistol grip
running pliers

1. SCORE GLASS

Use the pistol grip to score your intended cut. Keep your wrist up and hold the pistol grip perpendicular to the glass. Starting at the top, press firmly and pull toward you, moving the pistol grip with even pressure. Don't let go and start again on the same line. (You can also start at the bottom of the glass, scoring away from you if that feels most comfortable.)

2. BREAK INTO PIECES

One side of the running pliers will have a small, engraved line on it—this is meant to line up with your score line. Squeeze the pliers to give them the leverage needed to make the score line pop. Use your other hand to hold onto the length of the glass while it snaps.

RHAJAD'S CARPET

On this light switch plate—created by my daughter Kiah—you can see various cuts of tile. She cut ¾" (2cm) orange and white tiles in half using the Point, Pinch, Pop method. She did the same to create the gold triangles. The small white and orange squares are rectangles cut once more into squares. She created the blue "fringe" with outlines.

Chapter 2

A Visual Feast

SAMPLE PATTERNS COMBINING MILLEFIORI AND TILE

During my mosaic workshops, many students photograph my work inch by inch, wanting to remember the exact patterns I used. It is this desire that sparked the idea to create a book showcasing millefiori techniques along with patterns for easy reference—like an embroidery or quilting book filled with different patterns.

In this chapter, I have assembled more than fifty of the simple patterns that I use most frequently. I know there are dozens more, but I had to leave something for the sequel to this book! I have also included ten examples of more complex patterns for additional reference, and I've added six large combined patterns for inspiration.

Patterns are made up of individual tiles in varying shapes that fit together in rows to form a whole. One thing to remember when choosing patterns is to avoid getting caught up with what you see—the tiles and patterns in their current shapes and sizes. You can always cut, dice, splice and rearrange tiles in the patterns to fit projects as needed.

Now you get the idea of what you'll find in this chapter: lots of possibilities and endless combinations! Keep in mind that the color batches and variations of tiles and millefiori are ever-changing, so you may not find exactly what you see here. Or you may find a pattern you like and use it over and over again, and then a color will be discontinued. As much as we hate to see a favorite tile go, there will be other wonderful bits and pieces to take its place. My motto? Always use the good stuff. You can't keep it forever, so use it!

How to Set a Pattern

Possibilities for pattern arrangements are endless. But regardless of what pattern you choose, if you tile a length longer than a few inches, you have a couple of ways to go about setting the pattern. The method you choose is a personal preference; people see sections of patterns differently in their minds.

One way to set a pattern is row by row. Most designs in the projects are made of several rows, such as a row of cut rectangles, a row of millefiori and a row of triangles. So to set a pattern row by row, you do just that: Set the first row (e.g., cut rectangles) then the middle row (e.g., millefiori and the final row, like triangles).

The other way to set a pattern is in block areas, which is the way I generally do it because I see the patterns in blocks rather than rows. I work everything faster that way, but you may be different. If you choose to set a pattern in blocks, you would set all the rows at once, in small sections. For example, you would set about a 2–4" (4–6cm) area of pattern (cut rectangles, millefiori and triangles). Then you would set another 2–4" (4–6cm) section of pattern, and so on.

When choosing a method, go with what looks easier to you at first glance. There is a flow to doing mosaics, like doing Tai Chi. There is a rhythm to the setting: pick up, set, place, pick up, set, place ... Feel the movement. Your cutting and setting will be a bit choppy at first, but eventually you will find your rhythm and go with the flow.

ROWS OR BLOCKS?

The method you choose for setting patterns is personal preference. So when choosing a method, go with what strikes you at first glance. Take a look at these samples. Do you see the patterns as rows, blocks or both?

Simple Patterns

The simple patterns are just that—simple. They're comprised of just one or two rows of tiles. Individually, they make beautiful additions to any project. Start a pattern as shown and then continue it as long as you need. The patterns' simplicity also allows them to be easily combined with other patterns to create more complex patterns. Don't know which pattern to choose? The patterns are organized by color so decide what palette you like first. Then pay attention to how each pattern makes you feel and choose the one you love!

Millefiori Patterns

Below are a few simple patterns combining varying sizes and cuts of millefiori. These patterns show how much variety you can acheive with just millefiori!

SIMPLE PATTERN 1

SIMPLE PATTERN 2

SIMPLE PATTERN 3

SIMPLE PATTERN 4

SIMPLE PATTERN 5

SIMPLE PATTERN 6

SIMPLE PATTERN 7

SIMPLE PATTERN 8

SIMPLE PATTERN 9

SIMPLE PATTERN 10

SIMPLE PATTERN 11

SIMPLE PATTERN 12

SIMPLE PATTERN 13

SIMPLE PATTERN 14

Tile and Millefiori Patterns

Here are several simple patterns combining varying sizes and cuts of millefiori along with different shapes of tile. These patterns show how the possibilities are nearly endless!

SIMPLE PATTERN 15

SIMPLE PATTERN 16

SIMPLE PATTERN 17

SIMPLE PATTERN 18

SIMPLE PATTERN 19

SIMPLE PATTERN 20

SIMPLE PATTERN 21

SIMPLE PATTERN 22

SIMPLE
PATTERN 23

SIMPLE
PATTERN 24

SIMPLE
PATTERN 25

SIMPLE
PATTERN 26

SIMPLE
PATTERN 27

SIMPLE
PATTERN 28

SIMPLE
PATTERN 29

SIMPLE
PATTERN 30

SIMPLE
PATTERN 31

SIMPLE
PATTERN 32

SIMPLE
PATTERN 33

SIMPLE
PATTERN 34

SIMPLE
PATTERN 35

SIMPLE
PATTERN 36

SIMPLE
PATTERN 37

SIMPLE
PATTERN 38

SIMPLE
PATTERN 39

SIMPLE
PATTERN 40

SIMPLE
PATTERN 41

SIMPLE
PATTERN 42

SIMPLE
PATTERN 43

SIMPLE
PATTERN 44

SIMPLE
PATTERN 45

SIMPLE
PATTERN 46

SIMPLE PATTERN 47

SIMPLE PATTERN 48

SIMPLE PATTERN 49

SIMPLE PATTERN 50

SIMPLE PATTERN 51

SIMPLE PATTERN 52

SIMPLE PATTERN 53

SIMPLE PATTERN 54

SIMPLE PATTERN 55

SIMPLE PATTERN 56

SIMPLE PATTERN 57

SIMPLE PATTERN 58

Millefiori and the Weather

What does millefiori have to do with the weather, you might wonder? Well, just like the weather, millefiori designs come and go. My advice: When you see a pattern and color you like, buy it. I'm not saying millefiori is hard to get; it is just that finding the same pattern twice may be a challenge. There are hundreds of patterns made, but consistency is difficult to achieve.

Colors are unstable when heated to molten-hot and then cooled. Recipes and mixing can also be a factor. My suggestion to you is to pay more attention to the size and shape of the millefiori that I have selected for these patterns (and for the projects in chapter 3). These are much more important than the designs and colors I have used. Choose designs and colors that work within your own palette of choice. And don't get too attached to a particular millefiori design you see here. Remember, they come and go like the weather.

Complex Patterns

I have grouped simple patterns together to form larger, more complex patterns. These complex patterns show how the simple patterns can be combined, and how you can add to them (for example, changing the colors, adding gems or setting rosettes) to create more intricate designs. These complex patterns are especially helpful to the beginner as it can be challenging to come up with an entire design on your own. Use these patterns in projects and then let them inspire your own!

COMPLEX
PATTERN 1

COMPLEX
PATTERN 2

COMPLEX PATTERN 4

COMPLEX PATTERN 5

COMPLEX PATTERN 6

COMPLEX PATTERN 7

COMPLEX PATTERN 8

COMPLEX PATTERN 9

COMPLEX PATTERN 10

COMPLEX PATTERN 11

Combined Patterns

These combined patterns are groupings of multiple simple and complex designs. These patterns show how you can build elaborate designs from simple pattern foundations. Plus, they are beautiful inspiration—a visual feast of millefiori and tile!

COMBINED PATTERN 1

COMBINED PATTERN 2

COMBINED PATTERN 3

COMBINED PATTERN 4

COMBINED PATTERN 5

COMBINED PATTERN 6

ISHRAM'S SCRY

Once different patterns are combined, it becomes like weaving a tapestry, one pattern leading into the next. As in a tapestry, it's important to consider the piece as a whole, how patterns work together. Using multiple patterns can make a piece look busy. Colorful is wonderful! But to avoid creating a completely overwhelming design, place simple, single rows of tile or long thin pieces of glass between more detailed patterns to give the eye a place to rest.

Chapter 3

Mosaic Renaissance

TEN MODERN PROJECTS TO CREATE

So, here we are: artistic engineers, fusing art, functionality and whimsy. The ten projects ahead are just that: practical and beautiful, whimsical and just for fun. I tried to open doors to a few of the creative ways you can use millefiori in mosaics. For as long as millefiori has been around and recorded, it's amazing we can still find new and exciting applications. I hope these projects, which start with tiling a basic trivet (page 44) and take you all the way to crashing glass (page 94), will inspire you, whether you are new to the craft or just in need of fresh ideas. You may not want to complete all the projects, or for that matter even like all that you see; but if there is just one idea here that excites you, my job is complete.

Some of the projects require cutting very small tiles and piecing tiles very closely together. If you are just beginning to get into the world of mosaics, do not be discouraged! You can work a little larger or leave more grout space between your tile pieces. Do it your way, at your level, and it will still make for a fun, unique piece.

My intention is for no one to take my designs and tesserae choices too seriously. They are meant to inspire ideas and help get you started. Please (I beg!) make these mosaics your own. If you can't find a material I used in a particular project, don't stress, just improvise! The world is chock-full of goodies to work with. In fact, the What You'll Need lists for each project do not include specific colors or types of tiles for this reason; they simply indicate the size and shape of tiles you need and how many colors to complete the design I used. For that matter, don't even limit yourself to my designs; check out all the sample patterns in chapter 2! The important thing to learn from this chapter is how you build the designs. The patterns are just suggestions. No two mosaics are ever alike. Amen to that!

As old an art form as mosaics is, we have only just begun! These projects are by no means the end-all in mosaics; they are just a few more ways to play the fields millefiori style!

Tappetino Trivet

In its most practical form, this richly patterned square is a trivet ready to use as a hot plate for your next meal. But I call it *tappetino* (Italian for "little rug") because it reminds me of a miniature tapestry rug for adorning tables and walls. As pieces of art, you can scatter trivets such as this about the house like tiny decorative rugs. Sit one atop an ottoman, hang another on a wall, adorn the coffee table, even decorate the floor of your hamster's cage. As they are small and square, *tappentini* are a great introduction to crafting mosaics with millefiori and richly colored tiles. You'll get to practice all the basics: cutting tiles, priming, grouting and laying basic patterns. After mastering this one *tappetino*, you'll be weaving your own style of beautiful tapestries.

WHAT YOU'LL NEED:

Tesserae (see page 18)*

cut tiles: medium triangles (3 colors), rectangles (4 colors), thin rectangles (outlines) (1 color), small rectangles (1 color), small squares (1 color)

millefiori (whole slices and half-cuts)

Tools and Materials

wheeled glass cutters and/or tile nippers

plywood about 6" × 6" (15cm × 15cm)

Priming Kit (p. 15)

ruler or straightedge

permanent marker

tinted mastic (p. 14)

tweezers

palette knife

copper foil tape (⅜" [1cm])

copper head tacks

hammer

Grouting Kit (p. 16) (optional)

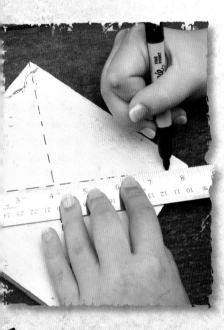  

1. PREPARE TRIVET

Prime the plywood (see Priming on page 15 as needed). It helps to mark the center of the design before tiling. Start by drawing two diagonal lines on the trivet using a permanent marker.

2. MARK THE CENTER

Mark off the center section by drawing a square using the intersection of the diagonal lines as the square's center. The square should be roughly 2" (5cm) wide.

3. START TILING CENTER

Spread mastic to cover the center square. (See Spreading Mastic on page 15 as needed.) Then begin setting your center design. Start by setting a millefiori rosette (see page 19 as needed). Surround each side of the rosette with a small cut triangle. Surround that diamond shape with four medium cut triangles in a different color.

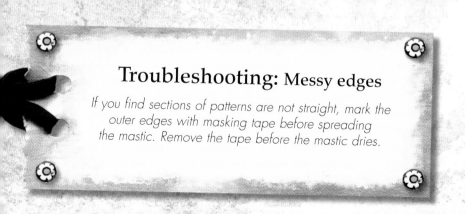

Troubleshooting: Messy edges

If you find sections of patterns are not straight, mark the outer edges with masking tape before spreading the mastic. Remove the tape before the mastic dries.

*See pages 18–22 for a description of cut tiles and instructions for cutting.

4. BUILD ROWS AROUND CENTER

Working out from the center, lay simple borders around the trivet. Spread mastic in sections. Here, I set the following five rows: (1) alternating rectangles and millefiori; (2) thin rectangle outlines (see page 22 as needed); (3) alternating rectangles and millefiori; (4) alternating rectangles and millefiori; (5) alternating small rectangles and small squares. (See How to Set a Pattern on page 26 as needed.)

5. TILE EDGE OF TRIVET

Set the last three rows along the outer border of the trivet. In the first row, alternate cut rectangles with millefiori. Then alternate medium triangles in two colors. Finally, alternate more rectangles with millefiori.

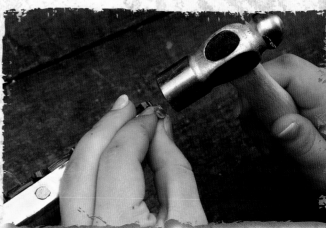

6. APPLY COPPER TAPE

Apply the copper foil tape to the sides of the trivet. Line the top edge of the tape with the top edge of the wood (rather than the top of the tiles). Wrap the excess underneath the trivet to secure it. At the corners, cut a slit in the tape before folding it under so you get a neat corner.

7. ADD COPPER TACKS TO SIDE OF TRIVET

Copper head tacks are a nice finishing accent and also help to secure the copper tape. Hammer about three tacks into each side of the trivet. If you plan on hanging the trivet, you don't need to grout the piece if you prefer (see sidebar on the next page). Just add a small hook to the back to finish. If the trivet will be handled a lot or used as a hot plate, grout the trivet. (See page 17 as needed.) Let the mastic dry for twenty-four hours before grouting (if you choose to grout).

To Grout or Not to Grout?

Not every mosaic project requires grouting. The textural variety of millefiori and smalti is part of their beauty, and not grouting allows you to enhance the mosaic by exposing the edges, often revealing colors and textures that would not otherwise be seen. But grouting protects the tiles, holding delicate pieces in place and securing corners and edges. So how do you decide to grout or not? Consider two factors:

Environment. Where is your finished piece going? If the piece will be outside or exposed to water (such as a backsplash or art hung in a bathroom), it should be grouted.

Purpose. How will the piece be used? If a project will hang on a wall or be displayed on a shelf, like a mirror or bottle, grouting is not necessary. However, if the piece will have a functional purpose, like a trivet or light switch plate, or if it will be handled a lot, like a box, grouting provides stability.

TAPPENTINO WITH FRINGE

I tiled this trivet to look like a miniature rug, complete with fringe. The green thin rectangle outlines alternating with larger cuts of off-white stained glass create the fringe effect. This trivet is also a great example of using found objects for embellishment. Rhinestone pieces make nice corner accents, and a rhinestone chain set face down frames the center.

TAPPENTINO WITH CUPID

I can't seem to get enough of rhinestone chain because I used it again on this trivet. Set face down, the tiny tracks of gold provide perfect frames for the millefiori rosettes. For the centerpiece, I placed glass over a vintage photo and framed it with ball chain. This method of making personalized photo tiles adds a new dimension to the art of mosaics.

Placche per Interruttori
Light Switch Plates

Once you see the light, the days of dull beige light switch plates will be gone! Sparkling mosaic switch plates are a great way to add richness and style around the house. Plus, they make great little treasures to give as unique gifts. Since the time my daughter was ten years old, we would sit around the table making her teachers' gifts as part of holiday traditions and end-of-the-year good-byes. Homemade gifts are always the best, but some occasions call for easy and quick! The good news is you can quickly craft a mosaic like these light switch plates. I will show you how to make three distinct styles, so you can surely find one that is right for anyone.

WHAT YOU'LL NEED:

Tesserae (see page 18)

Simple Switch Plate
cut tiles: small rectangles (1 color), small squares (1 color)

whole tile (1 color)

Contemporary Switch Plate
cut tiles: thin rectangles (2 colors), very small squares (1 color)

miscellaneous pieces of tile

stained glass pieces (2–3 colors)

millefiori (whole slices)

beads or flat-backed marbles (optional)

Moroccan Switch Plate
cut tiles: large triangles (1 color), medium triangles and small triangles (1 color), thin rectangles (2 colors), small squares (1 color)

whole tile (1 color)

millefiori (whole slices and half-cuts)

stained glass pieces (2 colors)

Tools and Materials

wheeled glass cutters and/or tile nippers

three switch plates and six 1"(3cm) screws

Priming Kit (p. 15)

tweezers

masking tape (optional)

mastic (untinted and tinted [see p. 14])

palette knife

copper foil tape (⅜" [1cm])

permanent marker

running pliers

Grouting Kit (see p. 16)

skewer

Semplice *Simple Switch Plate*

1. PRIME AND SPREAD UNTINTED MASTIC

Prime the switch plate (see Priming on page 15 as needed). Spread a thin layer of untinted mastic around the opening of the switch plate. (You will not embed millefiori in this design, so thick mastic is not required.) Spread the mastic about the width of your small square tiles.

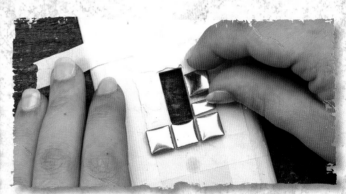

2. SET TILES AROUND OPENING

Place tiles around the opening, alternating small squares and very small rectangles (if needed to fill space). Be sure to leave slight spaces between each tile for grout. Place the tiles flush with the inside edge of the switch hole; be careful not to extend tiles into the hole or your switch won't fit.

3. FINISH SETTING CENTER DESIGN

Place tiles snugly around screw holes, but leave enough room for the screw heads. Place three ceramic tiles around the top hole (two next to it and one just above it). Fill in the remaining space with two triangles and a thin rectangle. Complete the same pattern at the opposite end of the switch plate.

4. ADD TILES TO SIDES OF PLATE

Spread mastic along one side of the switch plate and place whole tiles on that side. Cut rectangles as needed to fill space. Also, place your tiles so that they do not stop at the beveled edge of the switch plate but hang over sightly (to be flush with the back of the plate).

5. CHECK PLACEMENT OF TILES

Turn the switch plate over to check the placement of the tiles (over the edge). Then complete the other side of the switch plate as you did in step 4.

6. CUT AND PLACE TRIANGLES

Set two large triangles to fill in the remaining space. If they overlap, miter-cut the corners for a perfect fit. Set one tile in the mastic, then place the other tile in its spot, and mark the part that overlaps. Cut that piece off and place the triangle.

7. ADD COPPER TAPE

Scrape off any dried mastic along the edges of the switch plate. Then place copper tape around the edges. Place the tape just underneath the tiles, then fold over the edge and secure on the back. Make a small slit at the corners to create a neat fold. Press your thumb along the edge for a smooth, secure fit.

8. GROUT SWITCH PLATE

Let the mastic dry for 24 hours before grouting. Grout the switch plate. (See page 17 as needed.) Pay careful attention to the edges of the switch plate; use your index finger and thumb to work the grout into the space between the tiles and the edge of the switch plate.

9. PIERCE HOLES IN GROUT FOR SCREWS

Poke a hole where the screw holes are while the grout is still wet using a skewer (or other thin, sharp tool). Dip the skewer in water and allow a drop from the tip to fall over the grouted hole, softening that spot. Insert the skewer and rotate in a circular motion. Blow through the hole to remove any grout chunks.

Contemporaneo *Contemporary Switch Plate*

1. SET TILES AROUND OPENING

Prime the switch plate. Then spread a layer of tinted mastic around the opening. Place one thin rectangle on each of the four sides of the switch hole. Don't extend the tiles into the hole. Then set two more thin rectangles in another color, one on the left side and one on the right side of the hole. Fill the corners with very small squares.

2. DRAW ABSTRACT DESIGN

Draw a free-form abstract design on the switch plate. Cut your stained glass into smaller pieces, using the pen design as a guide for what sizes and shapes to cut. (See Cutting Stained Glass on page 23 as needed.) You can also use cut glass tiles to fill in small sections of the design.

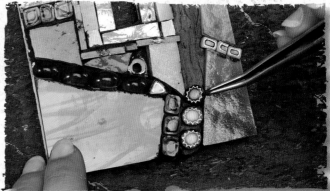

3. SET STAINED GLASS PIECES

Spread a layer of mastic thick enough for embedding millefiori over the switch plate (see Spreading Mastic on page 15 as needed). Set the pieces of glass, leaving spaces between the pieces to fit rows of millefiori.

4. PLACE MILLEFIORI, ADD COPPER TAPE, GROUT

Set rows of different millefiori into the spaces. Large beads or flat-backed marbles also work well as a filler. Cut the marbles or beads in half and set the cut side into the mastic. (These can be cut with wheeled glass cutters.) Fill in any odd remaining spaces with scrap glass, cut to fit. (Make sure you don't cover the screw holes.) Follow steps 7–9 from the Simple Switch Plate to add copper tape and grout.

Troubleshooting: Tiles that won't stick

Vitreous glass tiles have ridges on the bottom, so they can be fussy about sticking when you're using just a thin layer of mastic. To ensure that they are grabbing well, pop one off and check if the mastic went into the grooves of the ridges. If not, you know you need a thicker layer of mastic. Have no fear if you use too much: Just clean out the spaces with a craft knife after the mastic has set for a couple of hours.

Marocchino *Moroccan Switch Plate*

1. PLACE TILES AROUND OPENING

Prime the switch plate. Then spread a layer of tinted mastic around the opening. Place four triangles in the same color around the center hole. You'll need two medium and two small triangles. You will likely need to snip off the points of the medium triangles for all four pieces to fit.

2. BUILD ROWS AROUND CENTER DESIGN

Build rows around the center design in wide sections (see How to Set a Pattern on page 26). You can mark out your sections in permanent marker if you prefer. Spread a thick layer of mastic in the first section and then place five rows: (1) thin rectangle outlines (2) millefiori *di profilo* with cut side facing the switch; (3) millefiori (don't cover the screw holes); (4) a row of millefiori *di profilo* with cut side facing the switch; (5) a row of thin rectangle outlines.

3. CONTINUE SETTING ROWS

Spread a thick layer of mastic in the second section. Start setting a row alternating small squares with millefiori. Cut the tiles into triangles if needed to fit in along the left and right edges of the switch plate. Then set another row of thin rectangle outlines.

4. PLACE CORNER PATTERNS, ADD TAPE, GROUT

Repeat the same pattern in the four corner areas of the switch plate: Place two large triangles next to the row of outlines. (Remember to place tiles slightly beyond the edge of the switch plate.) Then place a whole tile in the corner. Fill in the space with thin rectangle outlines (cut to fit as needed). Follow steps 7–9 from the Simple Switch Plate to add copper tape and grout.

RAJASTHANI DESIGN

More than just tiles (actually, I used very few tiles here) went into making this switch plate. It is a mixture of fabric beaded trims (around the edge), found jewels, millefiori, beads, pearls and gold tile (which is cut to frame the center of the switch).

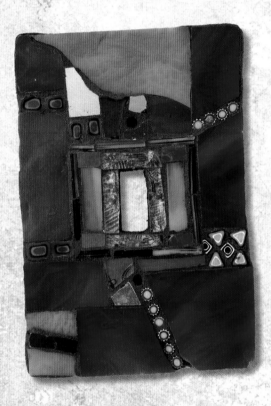

ABSTRACT IN RED

This is an elegant yet funky light switch plate made with large pieces of stained glass cut randomly. The larger glass sections are interspersed with flowing rows of millefiori. Stained glass and gold outline the center of the switch plate and gives it an even inside edge. Instead of featuring individual patterns pieced together, this mosaic is fluid and the entire switch plate is a single pattern.

OLD BRASS PLATES

A simple switch plate—made from gold, millefiori and van Gogh glass—gets a twist with the addition of brass bookplates. The plates frame small pieces of book pages. Incorporating such unique items like these brass plates, as well as beads, found objects and trims, lend texture and pizzazz to any basic mosaic. My daughter, Kiah created this switch plate.

54

At Home

Entering a World of Her Own Creation

My daughter writes, "My mother lives in a world of her own creation. You walk in her house and to some it is jaw-dropping; to others, it is cluttered and bewildering; a museum, full of mosaics. To her friends it is beautiful, if not a bit surreal."

The photo to the left shows the entranceway into Laurel Skye Design. An entrance really sets the tone of what is to come; it creates a transitional space allowing visitors to feel as though they are stepping into a new experience. And this one certainly does that.

This entrance is a cornucopia of tiles. The walls and benches are tiled with large Mexican tiles cut with a wet saw. But the wall's centerpiece mosaic—tiled over an attached board of the same shape—is a combination of glass, iridium and millefiori, all cut with a handheld wheeled glass cutter. The leg that supports the bench is also laiden in millefiori. The floor is tiled in a Moroccan-inspired fashion and is a colorful mix of vitreous glass and ceramic. Dark blue cove tiles finish the outer edge of the floor. So in all, the entrance to my studio reflects the detail of a Moroccan floor set within a Mexican cantina. Go figure.

(Left) The entrance to Laurel Skye Designs.

Scatole Simple Box

A treasure chest conjures thoughts of jewels of diamonds, gold and doubloons hidden within. But what if we can take our ordinary boxes and encrust them with gold tiles and beads and let the box be the treasure itself? This simple jeweled box was actually born out of a need to house my tiny finds. (The title "mosaic artist" legitimizes my quest to gather all the trinkets of the world.) I kept this box simple for easy tiling for those at the beginning of their mosaic journey. But after a box or two think "outside the box," and begin adding all kinds of dimensional treasures.

WHAT YOU'LL NEED:

Tesserae (see page 18)

cut tiles: medium triangles (3 colors), rectangles (4 colors), thin rectangles (outlines) (1 color), small rectangles (1 color), small squares (1 color)

millefiori (whole slices and half-cuts)

Tools and Materials

wheeled glass cutters and/or tile nippers

wood box with hinged lid

Priming Kit (p. 15)

palette knife

tinted mastic (p. 14)

tweezers

Grouting Kit (p. 16) (optional)

1. SPREAD MASTIC

Prime the box (see Priming on page 15 as needed). Set the box so that the front is facing up (and hinges are set on the work surface). Using the palette knife, spread mastic along the top edge of the lid. (See Spreading Mastic on page 15 as needed.)

2. SET TILE ALONG TOP EDGE OF LID

Set tiles into the mastic. Alternate small rectangles with very small squares. Remember to place the tiles close together.

3. FILL IN REST OF LID; SET MIDDLE ROW

Set the remaining two rows to fill in the side of the lid. (See How to Set a Pattern on page 26 as needed.) For the middle, place small squares at a diagonal. Then fill in the remaining spaces with small triangles. (This pattern is called a diamond tessellation.) Cut triangles smaller as needed to fit the space.

4. FILL IN REST OF LID; SET BOTTOM ROW

For the bottom row, alternate rectangles with millefiori. Be sure to set the pieces flush with the bottom of the lid so it will close properly. Complete steps 1–4 to fill in the other three sides of the lid.

5. ADD TILE TO PERIMETER OF TOP

It's time to fill in the top of the box. Start placing the row along the perimeter of the box. Spread a thin layer of mastic in small sections, alternating small squares and small rectangles. It's very important to overlap the tiles on the top edge of the lid so they are flush with the edge of the tiles on the side of the lid.

6. ADD MORE ROWS TO BOX TOP

Set three more rows on the lid, (1) small rectangles; (2) diamond tessellation using small squares and small triangles; (3) small rectangles. Fill extra spaces with very small triangles.

BLUSHING BRIDE'S BOX

The original "blushing bride" (on which I based the mosaic skull on page 90) was named Marianne Primack, a child of wealth in the early 1600s. She grew up in love with a farmhand who worked for her family. At sixteen, Marianne was torn away from her lover to be married to a ruthless businessman. She kept in a beautiful box, secreted away from prying eyes, letters that she and her lover exchanged. The last letter from him stated his hope to find a way to be with her forever before she was forced into a dreaded marriage. She wrote for him to meet her at a chapel outside of town, but the letter was intercepted. Marianne waited at the altar for her lover, who never came. The box of letters was discarded and later found at the bottom of the sea. This is my mosaic rendition of that box.

7. SET CENTER OF TOP

Begin the center of the top by spreading mastic over the entire area. Place three groupings of small squares set like diamonds (to form larger diamond shapes). The two groups at the sides should have three squares and one triangle (along the outer edge). The center group should have four squares. When setting the squares, leave space in between to set millefiori.

8. SET MILLEFIORI IN CENTER PATTERN

Use small and medium triangles to fill in the spaces between the three groupings. Fill in the spaces between the individual tiles with millefiori.

9. TILE BOTTOM OF BOX

Start tiling the bottom portion of box, starting with the two shorter sides. Just under the lid, place a thin row, alternating rectangles with very small squares. Below that, place a row alternating rectangles, small squares and framed millefiori (a millefiori surrounded by four very small triangles.) Place the bottom row using two colors of thin rectangles, alternating several rectangles with a column of millefiori. Then repeat these rows to tile the front and back of the box, placing tiles at the corners flush with each other.

10. GROUT BOX

Let the mastic dry for 24 hours before grouting. Grout the box. (See page 17 as needed.) Start working grout into the top of the box, then move onto the sides and then the front and back. Be sure to lift the lid to get in all those edges.

Troubleshooting: Falling tiles

If a tile falls off during grouting, you can't just use the wet grout stick it back into place. (Remember, grouting is cohesive not an adhesive.) Stop grouting, clean the area and find the tile or recut one. Then readhere it with adhesive like mastic, liquid nails or silicone. Then you can continue to grout, need I say "carefully," around that spot.

Tessuto di Vetro
Tapestry Mirror

People often ask me what my favorite project is and my answer is always the one I'm working on at the moment—that's the one I have thrown myself into completely and that gets all my attention, juice and passion. That said, I do love functional art; and as utilitarian art goes, there aren't many surfaces more beautiful than a mirror framed in mosaic tiles. I think of my mosaic mirrors as jewelry for the walls. *Tessuto di vetro* literally translates into "woven glass." Why call it that? We will weave a tapestry around our mirrors, using tile and glass as our fabric and millefiori as our thread. And since this mirror will hang safely on the wall, no grouting is needed, allowing the wonderful texture and color along the edges to take center stage.

Honorable Mention: Two of the greatest pioneers in this method are Dusciana Bravura and her father, Marco Bravura.

WHAT YOU'LL NEED:

Tesserae (see page 18)

cut tiles: enough to complete 10 simple patterns (see pages 27-34 for ideas) and 9 complex patterns (see pages 35-37 for ideas), small rectangles

millefiori (whole slices)

Tools and Materials

unfinished, wood-framed mirror
(with a 2" [5cm] frame)

wheeled glass cutters and/or tile nippers

hook, nails, hammer (optional)

scrap cardboard (size of mirror)

Priming Kit (p. 15)

hollow copper rods

tin snips

22-gauge copper wire

masking tape (optional)

tinted mastic (p. 14)

palette knife

running pliers

tweezers

acrylic metallic paint

paintbrush

1. ATTACH HARDWARE AND PRIME

If your mirror needs a hook, attach it first. Also, cut and place a piece of scrap cardboard over the mirror to protect it. You can add masking tape to the edges of the frame to protect them from messy mastic application, if desired. Then prime the mirror frame (see Priming on page 15 as needed).

2. MEASURE AND CUT COPPER ROD

Before you begin tiling, cut and prepare the hollow copper rods. Place a copper rod across the frame to determine the width. Use tin snips to cut and crimp the end of the copper rod. Repeat steps 2 and 3 to cut additional copper rod pieces.

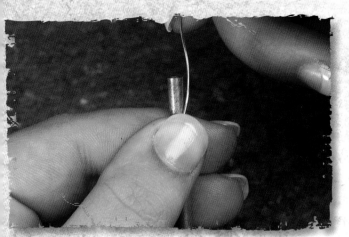

3. START WIRE WRAP

Wrap the copper wire around the rod. (The wire will help the rod cling to the mastic.) Stretch the wire down the rod about 1" (3cm) and hold the end of the wire secure with your thumb.

4. FINISH WRAPPING WIRE AROUND ROD

Wrap the long end of the wire around the short end (against the rod) to secure it in place. Then wrap the wire down the rod to the end.

5. FINISH WRAPPING AND SNIP OTHER END

Using tin snips, cut through the tube and the wire, crimping the end. Bury the cut end of the wire in the mastic when you set the tube.

6. BEGIN FIRST COMPLEX PATTERN IN CORNER

The design of the frame is built from several simple and complex patterns of your choosing. Start building the frame's design in one corner. Spread mastic (see Spreading Mastic on page 15 as needed) and then set the first complex pattern, starting with its border.

7. FINISH CORNER PATTERN

Complete the first complex pattern by filling in the center with tiles and millefiori. (Here I am setting thin rectangle outlines, but your pattern will likely be different.)

8. COMPLETE TILING THE BOTTOM OF FRAME

From the corner, tile along the bottom side of the frame. Alternate simple patterns and complex patterns. Use rows of cut rectangles and/or millefiori for filler as needed. Remember to set borders of the complex patterns first, then their centers.

Troubleshooting: An uneven bedding

Keeping a level surface can be difficult for the beginner. Here are some simple tips for getting an even bedding:

- As you set the tiles, take care not to squish them in too far.
- Set your thicker millefiori and tiles deeper into the mastic and set thinner ones closer to the surface.
- Bury ragged and sharp edges down into the mastic.
- Place concave edges of millefiori face down and the flat sides face up.
- Spread mastic evenly. Make sure there is not too much in the center of a substrate and not enough at the edges.

9. TILE SIDES AND PLACE COPPER RODS

Complete the top side of the frame as you did the bottom. Then complete the side in the same manner. However, set your copper rods in between some patterns. Take care with the thickness of mastic you spread for the rods; it should be thick enough to embed them.

10. PAINT EDGE OF FRAME

Before the mastic dries, remove the protective cardboard from the mirror and remove any masking tape. Clean away unwanted mastic along the edge of the frame using a craft knife. After the mastic dries and tiles are set, you can clean unwanted mastic from the tiles. Then paint the edge of your frame with the acrylic paint. You don't need to grout the mirror—this piece is all about texture!

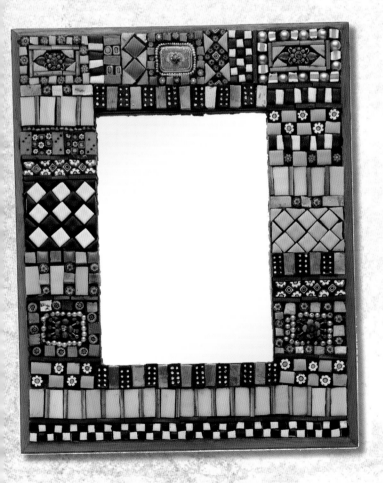

JOE'S DINER

I created this mirror with opaque ceramic tiles to give it a look reminiscent of a 1950s diner—a bit kitsch and a lot retro. Millefiori and other glass tesserae still made their way onto the frame, but the shiny ceramic tiles take center stage in the design. Much of the ceramic makes checkerboard or diamond patterns, recalling those old black-and-white diner floors. Small dominoes are used like tiles, again to recall the nifty fifties. Pearls and small jeweled flowers are wonderful to have on hand for this style of tiling because they can go just about anywhere to add texture and softness.

64

At Home

Stopping in Their Tracks

Thousands of feet have tread back and forth over this beautiful mosaic floor that leads to the sales room in Laurel Skye Designs—and it is still as intact as ever.

A simple mosaic installment can give any plain linoleum floor, like this one, a creative face lift (without the eventual sagging). I used many different kinds of mosaic tiles to set the pattern in this floor: vitreous glass, metallic vitreous glass, stained glass, iridium, gold ceramic and multicolored ceramic. I tiled it directly onto the floor (as opposed to tiling it indirectly, which I did on the bathtub you can see on page 88). Contrary to what you might think, the patterns of the tiny tiles are durable and easy to clean. And the glass reflects the light in ways solid ceramics can't.

This mosaic floor, created in several fortnights, was started simply with the border, a row at a time, then moving to the central diamonds and lastly, filling in between the center design and the border. The mosaic floor runner encompasses the entire six-foot-long walkway. As with most of my mosaic endeavors, I created the design as I laid it.

(Left) Hallway leading to the sales room in Laurel Skye Designs.

Specchio Vetro Decorato
Embellished Mirror

Literally, *vetro decorato* translates into "highly decorated in glass," but actually this mirror is just highly decorated! We will cross borders here into territory normally reserved for assemblage artists. Mosaic creation isn't just for tile-only projects. You can customize a mirror (or other piece of art) with personal items and found objects. And not much is off-limits for this embellished mirror: buttons, drawer pulls, bottle caps, old and broken jewelry, and coins all make their way onto the frame. Plus, adding soldered ball chain and patina will give your mirror the look of an antique collectible. So, why not add pretty gems to your project? We all look more beautiful reflected in a mirror framed in jewels!

Honorable Mention: Two of the many artists that inspired me in this method are Susan Gardner and Brian Sproul.

WHAT YOU'LL NEED:

Tesserae (see page 18)

cut tiles: large triangles (1 color)

other: millefiori (whole slices), piece of clear glass (about 1" × 2" [2cm × 5cm]), found objects, jewelry, cut glass and tile, copper rods, etc.

Tools and Materials

wheeled glass cutters and/or tile nippers

unfinished, wood-framed mirror (with a 2" [5cm] frame)

hook, nails, hammer (optional)

scrap cardboard (size of mirror)

Priming Kit (p. 15)

masking tape (optional)

copper foil tape (¼" [6mm])

flux paste and liquid flux

flux brush

100-watt soldering iron

solder (50/50)

brass ball chain

tweezers

sponge

liver of sulfur

paintbrush (for liver of sulfur)

bottle cap

two vintage photos (about 1" [2cm] square and 1" × 2" [2cm × 5cm])

pliers

scissors

silicone adhesive

glitter glue (two colors)

ball chain

dimensional gloss medium

permanent pen

tinted mastic (p. 14)

palette knife

pistol grip cutter

running pliers

veterinary syringe

craft stick

acrylic metallic paint

paintbrush

craft knife

1. PRIME AND ATTACH COPPER TAPE

If your mirror needs a hook, attach it first. Also place a piece of cardboard over the mirror to protect it. Then prime the mirror frame (see Priming on page 15 as needed). Cover the sides of the frame in masking tape. Then adhere copper foil tape along the outer edges of the frame, making sure the tape is secure.

2. BRUSH ON FLUX PASTE

Brush the flux paste on the copper tape using a flux brush. (You can cut the bristles at an angle for easier application.) The flux allows the solder to bind to the tape. Keep the flux on the tape; if it gets on the wood, the mastic won't adhere. You can apply masking tape to the inside of the frame before using the flux, if desired.

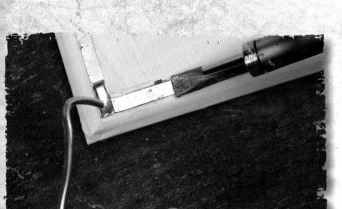

3. SOLDER OVER COPPER TAPE

Heat the soldering iron. (Be sure to have good ventilation or a fan blowing the vapors out toward an open door.) Then pull the solder along the copper tape using the iron to melt it. Think of the flux as subway rails and the solder as the train. The train will only go wherever the track takes it!

4. DIP BALL CHAIN IN LIQUID FLUX

Cut the ball chain into four pieces (to fit the four sides of the frame). Pour a small amount of liquid flux into a container and coat one piece of ball chain with the flux.

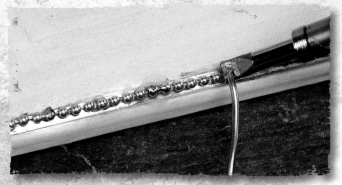

5. TACK COPPER CHAIN WITH SOLDER

Brush the already soldered copper tape with more flux paste (just one of the four frame sides). Use the tweezers to lay the chain over top. Then use the solder and iron to tack the chain to the frame in a few spots so it will stay in place during soldering. Touch the hot tip to the solder and the chain simultaneously, and let just a drop melt down onto the chain.

6. FINISH SOLDERING CHAIN

Flux the chain again using the flux paste. Guide and pull the melted solder along the chain, coating and securing the entire length of chain to a smooth finish. Remember, don't get discouraged; it takes practice to get the feel of how the solder moves.

7. APPLY LIVER OF SULFUR

Remove any masking tape on the inside of the frame. Clean off the flux from your frame using hot soapy water and a sponge. (There are also flux solvents available from stained glass suppliers.) Mix liver of sulfur with a bit of water, and then paint it along the ball chain and soldered metal to give it an aged look. Repeat steps 4–7 for the other three sides of the frame.

8. BEND BOTTLE CAP EDGES AND ATTACH PHOTO

Using a pair of pliers, bend out the fluted edge of the bottle cap. Cut your smaller photo to fit the inside of the bottle cap. Then adhere it using the silicone adhesive.

9. ADD GLITTER GLUE AND BALL CHAIN

Add glitter glue around the edge of the photo. Use the tweezers to set a 3" (8cm) length of ball chain in the glue.

10. ADD MORE GLITTER GLUE AND SEAL PHOTO

Add another color of glitter glue around the rim of the bottle cap. Then add dimensional gloss medium to the center of the bottle cap, covering the photo.

11. CUT CLEAR GLASS

Cut and size your rectangular photo to fit the frame. Then lay your piece of glass over the photo and outline an oval over the top of the glass with a permanent pen. Cut the glass (see Cutting Stained Glass on page 23) one small section at a time. Nibble any jagged edges with the wheeled glass cutters.

12. START SETTING OBJECT IN CORNER

You're ready to lay the mosaic! There is no specific pattern to set; just fill in the frame with found objects, glass, tiles, copper tubing and millefiori. Spread a layer of tinted mastic in the corner and begin placing objects. Use a thick enough layer to embed the pieces well. Add additional mastic directly to the piece (such as this jewel), if needed.

13. CREATE FOCAL POINT

Create a focal point at the top of the frame. Start with a large piece, like an old brooch, then shuffle around other found objects and cut tiles to create a pattern that frames the large object. Then continue adding mastic and pieces to fill in the top of the frame. (You can use a veterinary syringe to help get in tight corners.)

14. ATTACH PHOTO TO FRAME

Add mastic and objects to fill in the sides of the frame. To set your glass-covered photo, start by adhering the photo to the frame using the silicone adhesive.

BOTTLE CAP MILLEFIORI ART

Whether they are designs and patterns, or depicting scenes of nature, they are all the work of mosaic artist and mad scientist Josh Lowell. Most are made entirely with millefiori, cut from cane rod, melted, bent, pinched and stretched and then set into the backs of discarded bottle caps They are each a miniature art piece, reminiscent of classic paintings. These bottle caps have jump rings for use as jewelry, but I would love them for use in a gorgeous embellished mirror!

15. ADD SILICONE ADHESIVE TO GLASS

Add a big glob of silicone adhesive to the center of the glass. (If you spread the adhesive on the glass, you are likely to get air bubbles.)

16. PLACE GLASS AND REMOVE EXCESS ADHESIVE

Place the glass over the photo, allowing excess to ooze out to the edges. Use a craft stick to remove unwanted adhesive.

17. ADD MASTIC

Fill the syringe with mastic. (A syringe gives excellent control of application, unlike a squeeze bottle.) Fill in the areas around the photo with mastic.

18. PLACE MILLEFIORI

To help the oval fit into the rectangular area, place cut triangles in the four corners around the photo. Set millefiori all around the photo to frame it.

Working on an Easel

For mirror and picture frame mosaics, working on an easel can do three things:
1. Save your back and neck from straining
2. Allow you to see your piece vertically, as it will be seen when displayed
3. Help you to view it at a distance

With the vertical position of the frame, you can better examine your work. Ask yourself: Is the color balanced and flowing? Is it too busy in one area and not enough in another? Is it compositionally working? As you are working, stop often and back away or just leave the room. When you return, you can see your mirror on the easel from a distance, as others would see it for the first time walking into the room. If there is a section you are not happy with, either pop out the tiles (they can be washed) or scrape out the whole area and redo it. There is no right or wrong—just do what feels right for you, the artist.

19. FINISH MOSAIC

Fill in the bottom of the frame and any remaining blank spots. While mastic is still fresh, remove the center cardboard and masking tape. Use your fingertips to gently press everything into place and do any last-minute adjustments before the mastic dries.

20. PAINT FRAME EDGES

Paint the bare edges of the frame. I used a combination of gold and burnt umber paints. Allow the mastic and paint to dry. Then clean any mastic residue off the surface of the tiles with a craft knife.

MEXICAN MEMORY MIRROR

While in Puerto Vallarta, Mexico, I stumbled on a small scrap of orange glass while coming out of a charming little cantina at midnight, belly full of tortilla soup. The moon shone off its tattered surface and I picked it up and kept it, thinking "maybe I could use this someday." I schlepped it home to California. Three years later, there it was in my house, a reminder of a fabulous vacation. So I used it as the inspiration for this mirror. To this day, I cannot look at this mirror without my mouth watering for that soup!

Bottiglia Bottle

A cherished moment you have shared with someone over a bottle of wine can now live on with some mosaic intervention. In this project, an ordinary wine bottle is transformed into a piece of art with costume jewelry, soldering, ball chain, rhinestone, clear glass and, of course, millefiori. Bottles have to be one of the greatest mosaic surfaces you can use. After all, they are abundant, free and can be found in every imaginable shape and size. So pop off the cork on that bottle of merlot and follow me!

Honorable Mention: Jackie Iskander is a pioneer in creating mosaic bottles.

WHAT YOU'LL NEED:

Tesserae (see page 18)

cut tiles: thin rectangles (1 color), small rectangles (2 colors), very small squares (1 color), enough tiles for two simple patterns (see pages 27–34 for ideas)

millefiori (whole slices)

amber glass cut into ½" (1cm) squares

rhinestone chain (8" [20cm] long)

Tools and Materials

wheeled glass cutters and/or tile nippers

wine bottle

masking tape

copper tape (½" [1cm])

scissors

flux paste and liquid flux

flux brush

100-watt soldering iron

solder (50/50)

brass ball chain

liver of sulfur

tweezers

paintbrush (for liver of sulfur)

silicone adhesive

vintage photo
(about 2" × 3" [5cm × 8cm])

patterned paper (about 2¼" × 3¼")

Grouting Kit (p. 16)

1. ADHERE COPPER TAPE

Adhere copper foil tape around the lip of the bottle. Notch the tape at intervals and fold the edges of the tape into the bottle neck. Brush flux paste on the copper tape using a flux brush. Heat the soldering iron. Then pull the solder along the copper tape using the iron to melt it. (For more detailed information on soldering, see pages 67 and 68.)

2. SOLDER TAPE AND BALL CHAIN

Coat the ball chain with liquid flux. Brush the soldered copper tape with more flux paste. Using tweezers to lay the chain on top of the bottle, touch the hot tip to the solder and the chain simultaneously, coating the entire length of chain to a smooth finish. Wash the flux off completely using hot soapy water. Then brush liver of sulfur over the soldered metal to age it.

3. TILE BOTTOM OF BOTTLE

Tile the bottom of the bottle. Set two rows of very small squares about 1" (3cm) apart. In between the rows, alternate thin rectangles and a vertical row of millefiori. (See How to Set a Pattern on page 26.) Spread the silicone adhesive over a small area at a time (silicone dries quickly). Be careful that it doesn't ooze over the tiles—it is hard to clean after it dries.

4. TILE FRONT WITH TWO PATTERNS

Working vertically, set your design on the front bottom half of the bottle (above what you tiled in step 3). Start by placing a row of rectangles. Then place a simple pattern (see chapter 2) such as this blue-and-gold double tessellation.

5. FINISH BOTTOM FRONT OF BOTTLE

Place another row of rectangles. Then place a second simple pattern like this diamond tessellation. (I used four very small squares in two colors to act as my "diamonds.") Set a row of rectangles, then repeat the first pattern, then set a final row of rectangles. Now you should have the following vertical rows wrapping around the bottle: rectangles, first pattern, rectangles, second pattern, rectangles, first pattern, rectangles. Above these, set a horizontal row of very small squares.

6. TILE BACK OF BOTTLE

To tile the back of the bottle, repeat the vertical designs you started in steps 4 and 5, but this time tile all the way up, stopping just before the bottle starts to curve at the neck. Start by completing the two outer rows of rectangles (from steps 4 and 5) by tiling them all the way up. Then continue tiling: first pattern, rectangles, second pattern, rectangles, first pattern, and so on until the design wraps around the bottle. Fill in any empty spaces with tiles cut small to fit.

7. CUT AND ADHERE PHOTO AND PAPER

Adhere the vintage photo to the patterned paper; cut the final size to fit on the top front of the bottle. There should be enough room on either side to set two rows between the paper and the pattern on the back of the bottle. Affix the paper to the bottle using the silicone adhesive.

8. ATTACH AMBER GLASS TO PHOTO

Starting in one corner, cover the entire photo with the amber glass, placing the squares very close together (so that grout will not obscure the photo). To attach, put silicone adhesive on the back of each square and then press it to the photo.

9. TILE PHOTO BORDER

Set a row of very small squares around the sides and top of the photo. Next to that, place a border alternating rectangles and millefiori.

10. ADD ROWS OF TILE AT TOP

Above the design on the back of the bottle, set a row of small rectangles. Next place two rows of very small squares, making angled cuts where necessary to follow the curve of the bottle.

11. ATTACH RHINESTONE CHAIN

Nothing says luxury like a little glitz! Add a thin line of silicone adhesive just above the rows you placed in step 10. Using tweezers, set the chain of rhinestones in the adhesive.

12. TILE THE BOTTLE NECK

Finish by tiling up the neck to the crown. Start with three rows of small rectangles. Then set vertical rows, alternating a rectangle with millefiori (as in step 3). Place rows of small rectangles until you reach the top. Grout the bottle. (See page 17 as needed.)

Troubleshooting: Grout that won't stick

Add polymer additive (a whitish liquid) to the dry grout in place of water. This will help the grout stick better to the bottle. Polymer additive can also decrease the possibility of grout cracking. Grout with polymer additive dries faster, so you'll have to sponge it off more quickly than grout made with water alone.

A PLETHORA OF BOTTLES

Here are a few of my many mosaic bottles, once filled with wine, olive oil and milk (from left to right). What I love about doing bottles is that there is an endless supply of them. So many different sizes and shapes can be covered with mosaics, like whiskey bottles and jam jars and small glass apothecary bottles. Consider tiling unopened wine bottles or little olive jars with clear glass over the label, making two gifts in one!

At Home

Living With Mosaics

My mosaics don't just sit in my house—they live there. They are an integral part of the surrounding landscape of my spiritual center. They sit on pedestals, they adorn shelves in a hallway leading up to the sales room and workshop. A mosaic mask welcomes visitors who pass through the archway to the kitchen and a tiled light switch plate (to the left in this photo) replaces a drab plastic one and brightens the wall. The mosaic pieces that live in my home, along with all the other mismatched clutter and jewels that cover every inch of my unorthodox palace, create spaces that are rich with color and texture, weaving a tapestry of the world.

I am not a wealthy woman continuously buying expensive trinkets. But I am an expert scrounger and dumpster diver. As I wander, I am always alert to things around me that I might salvage. I will adopt just as easily a stray cat, a Tibetan nomad or a broken clock if our paths should cross and it needed a home. It is not what a thing is, so much as what I see it becoming; the vision of it becoming something more is what draws me to it. Taking something, whether whole or damaged, out of its ordinary context and infusing it with a new life, seeing it born again out of the rubble, is my calling. I guess you could call me something of a "rubble" rouser.

(Left) One of the many passageways in my home. I removed almost all the doors in the house so that the rooms flow into one another.

Ritratto fatto con Oggetti Trovatti
Found Objects Portrait

This project is reminiscent of the kitschy black velvet paintings I grew up with in California in the 1970s. My portrait is loosely styled from those paintings, but with a mosaic twist of course!

Found object portraits are a nice break from typical mosaics. There is very little cutting involved. I call this portrait *Our Lady of the Clutter* because it is a jumble of random pieces. It's time to open that drawer in the kitchen—you know the one—and start sorting out the old batteries, dice, the unclaimed checker piece, fishing bait (not live ones, please), that lost earring, a key (long forgotten what door it unlocks), a brass screw ... just about anything is fair game. Don't forget to grab a handful of millefiori; those sweet little patterned gems are perfect for filling in small spaces.

WHAT YOU'LL NEED:

Tesserae (see page 18)

found objects in brass and gold tones (e.g., old jewelry, coins, chains, trinkets, etc.)

millefiori (whole slices)

Tools and Materials

sculpting epoxy (like Magic Sculp)

paintbrush

acrylic paint in burnt sienna, crimson and gold (Golden)

tin snips

plastic bird and baby cake decorations

silicone adhesive

bronze acrylic paint

red heart sequin

picture frame

black cardstock (as large as frame)

ruler

craft knife or scissors

photocopy of a portrait

glue stick

clear-drying glue (MAC glue)

palette knife

black frit (ground glass), medium grit

1. SCULPT EPOXY SNAKE

To make a faux brass snake, roll out sculpting epoxy and coil into a snake. Let the epoxy harden overnight.

2. PAINT SNAKE

Paint the epoxy snake with a mix of burnt sienna and crimson acrylic paint. After that dries, highlight areas of the snake with gold acrylic paint.

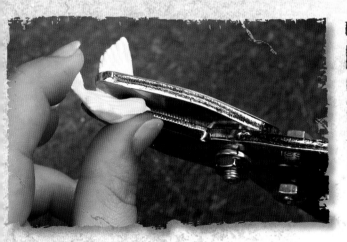

3. CUT OFF WINGS

To create a faux brass cherub, start by cutting off the wings of the plastic bird using the tin snips.

4. ATTACH WINGS TO BABY

Attach the wings to the back of the plastic baby using silicone adhesive. Allow the adhesive to dry.

5. PAINT CHERUB

Paint the cherub using bronze acrylic paint. When the paint has dried, adhere a sequin heart to the belly of the cherub using silicone adhesive. (Keep in mind that any other small plastic pieces you have also can be transformed into faux brass using this technique.)

6. MEASURE, CUT AND ATTACH CARDSTOCK

Measure and cut a piece of sturdy black cardstock to fit inside the frame. Using silicone adhesive, attach the cardstock over the glass in the frame.

7. CUT PHOTO AND ATTACH TO CARDSTOCK

Cut out your vintage photo and attach it to the cardstock using a strong-holding glue stick. Place the photo near the edge to allow plenty of room for the assemblage.

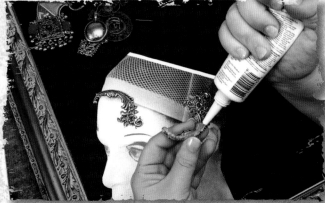

8. ADD LARGER OBJECTS ALONG HAIRLINE

Loosely arrange some of the larger found objects right along the hairline in the portrait. Attach the pieces using the silicone adhesive.

9. ADD MORE OBJECTS TO HAIRLINE AND EDGES

Add more objects close to the hairline and around the edges of the head.

10. FINISH ADDING FOUND OBJECTS

Continue adding found objects, including your handmade objects, building "hair" out from the portrait face.

11. PLACE MILLEFIORI AND FILL IN HOLES

When you are finished attaching found objects, set millefiori into the design using the adhesive. Fill in any holes with additional millefiori or pieces of chain.

12. SPREAD GLUE AND SPRINKLE WITH FRIT

Using a palette knife, spread clear-drying glue over the cardstock background (a section at a time). Generously sprinkle frit over the glue. When the background is covered, let the glue dry. Then blow off excess frit.

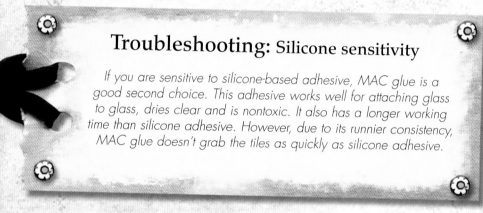

Troubleshooting: Silicone sensitivity

If you are sensitive to silicone-based adhesive, MAC glue is a good second choice. This adhesive works well for attaching glass to glass, dries clear and is nontoxic. It also has a longer working time than silicone adhesive. However, due to its runnier consistency, MAC glue doesn't grab the tiles as quickly as silicone adhesive.

PRINCESS OF ASIA

I love how many fun pieces are always lying around the house waiting to be put into a collage. Found object collage pieces don't have to be brass (or faux brass) to work. I created this portrait in red tones. The apple was last year's Christmas tree ornament. The gold piece at the top is the one remaining earring from a set my ex-husband gave me (the other half lost long ago, along with the marriage). A fabric flower, broken jewelry by way of yard sales and thrift shops, a few beads and millefiori, bright red dominoes and there you have it—a headdress fit for a princess! I assembled this piece with my daughter, Kiah.

Scarpa col Tacco High-Heeled Shoe

If the shoe fits, wear it. If it doesn't ... tile it! A shoe is a great way to strut your mosaic stuff. People are always asking me, "Is there a real shoe in there?!" I like to keep the magic a secret, but just between you and me, yes, there is. And I'm going to show you two ways to build that shoe: one using sculpting epoxy and one using gauze. The choice is yours. And this is one of those projects that greatly benefits from garage sale finds like half a pair of vintage earrings. After all, when you're making a glamorous high-heeled shoe you can really bring on the glitz and bling.

Honorable Mention: Two great pioneers in tiling shoes are Sharon Von Senden and Mindy Simbrat.

WHAT YOU'LL NEED:

Tesserae (see page 18)
cut tiles: very small squares (2 colors), small pieces (3 colors)

millefiori (whole slices and half-cuts)

costume jewelry

small ceramic plate

rhinestone chain

Tools and Materials

wheeled glass cutters and/or tile nippers

high-heeled shoe (backless, closed-toe)

sharp scissors

plaster of Paris

water

gloves

Covering shoe: Option A

two-part water soluble sculpting epoxy (Magic Sculp)

rolling pin

talcum powder

Covering shoe: Option B

plaster gauze

old scissors

water

black gesso

paintbrush

permanent pen
(or white chalk pencil)

silicone adhesive

hammer

towel

tweezers

Grouting Kit (p. 16)

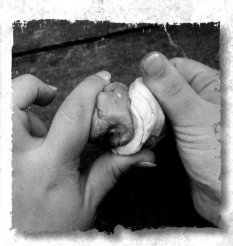

1. REMOVE SHOE STRAPS

Using sharp scissors, cut off any straps (cut close to the sole). If the shape of the upper is not quite right for you (for instance, if it's too high), you can cut a new shape since the shoe will be covered. Also remove any other thick elements like buckles.

2. STUFF TOE WITH PLASTER

Mix plaster of Paris with water to create a workable mud. Pack the plaster into the toe of the shoe and fill it completely. Smooth out the plaster so it transitions seamlessly from the upper to the instep, with just a slight dip. When you're finished, hang the shoe by the heel to dry until hard.

3. CHOOSE COVERING METHOD

There are two methods for covering the shoe: sculpting epoxy (Option A) and layering gauze (Option B). Sculpting epoxy (shown above) is what I prefer as it allows you to add elements like wings. But gauze is readily available at craft stores and some people prefer this method for that reason.

Looking for a Sensible Shoe

Keep your first shoe simple. I recommend starting with a simple mule (as I used for this project). A mule is a slip-on shoe, with the back open and the toes covered. A closed-toed shoe is best since an open toe is harder to plaster and tile.

The other consideration is what size to buy. Unless you plan to use your shoe to attack a midnight marauder or something, I recommend starting with a small shoe size because the shoe will gain a few sizes after tiling. Smaller tends to look better on display. On the other hand (or foot), if you hate cutting you might want to consider a larger shoe; you won't need to cut the tiles quite as small to fit.

Steps 4 and 5 (Covering Shoe): Option A, Sculpting Epoxy

4. MIX AND ROLL OUT SCULPTING EPOXY

Mix equal amounts of resin and hardener into a ball, and knead until the ball is well blended. Then roll out the epoxy until it's thin. You can add a little talcum powder if needed so the epoxy doesn't stick to the rolling pin.

5. COVER SHOE WITH SCULPTING EPOXY

Cover the entire shoe (including the heel and sole) with the rolled-out epoxy. Dampen the epoxy to smooth out lumps, and keep blending (using your fingers and/or a sponge) until you get an even coating. (Note: Objects like wings would be added at this point.) Allow the epoxy to set for 24 hours. Sculpting epoxy does not need a primer or sealer before tiling. The epoxy can be painted, so if you decide not to grout your shoe, you may want to paint it a color.

Steps 4 and 5 (Covering Shoe): Option B, Layering Gauze

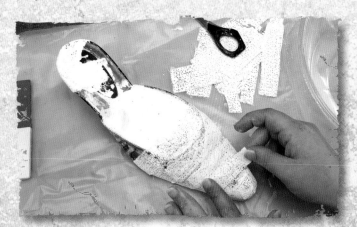

4. LAYER GAUZE OVER SHOE

Using old scissors, cut gauze into short strips about ½" (1cm) wide. Dip each strip in water, then start the first layer, slightly overlapping the strips. Cover the entire shoe (including the heel and sole). Add about three more layers, letting the gauze dry completely between layers. To speed up drying you can bake the shoe in the oven on 300 degrees until lightly golden.

5. PAINT GESSO OVER DRIED GAUZE

Brush gesso over the hardened gauze. You can use white gesso, but black makes it easier to see the tile design as you set it. And black looks nice as a background color if you leave the shoe ungrouted.

6. SET FOCAL POINT

When in doubt of where to start tiling, it's best to begin with a focal point. Set a piece of costume jewelry in the center of the shoe using silicone adhesive. It also helps to draw a rough plan for your design on the shoe. If you choose to do so, use a permanent pen (or a white chalk pencil if your shoe is painted black) to draw.

7. TILE BORDER OF SOLE

Start tiling with the border of the sole. Add a line of silicone adhesive to the shoe in small sections and place very small squares in a row.

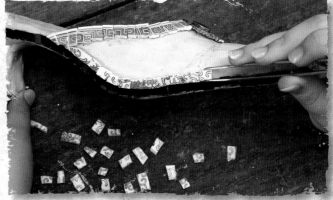

8. BREAK AND CUT PLATE

Place a plate face down inside a folded towel and hit with a hammer several times (as needed). Use the wheeled glass cutters to cut these pieces into smaller, more even pieces. Make sure you have some pieces cut from the rounded edge of the plate.

9. PLACE PIECES OF PLATE

Starting where the shoe's upper meets the sole, set the squares from the lip of the plate in a row along the edge of the upper. Stop when you reach the jewelry center piece. Repeat on the other side of the shoe. Then set the squares from the rest of the plate in a border above the tiles you set in step 7. Set the squares only on the upper (not the instep), starting where the upper and sole meet and continuing around the toe to the other side.

10. FILL IN UPPER

Fill in the rest of the upper part of the shoe with one color of tile. It's not necessary for the pieces to be cut evenly as long as they are similar in size. Pieces should be small enough to hug the curvature of the shoe. Also set a row of these same tiles, this time cut into very small squares, above the row you set in step 7 (along the instep).

11. ADD RHINESTONE CHAIN

Using tweezers and silicone adhesive, attach a rhinestone chain along the perimeter of the shoe. Start above the china plate pieces and continue all the way around the instep and heel, and back to where you began. This will help smooth the transition from tiling the upper to the instep.

12. SET MILLEFIORI ROSETTES

Add 3–5 spots of silicone adhesive (no bigger than a dime) to the instep of the shoe and then set millefiori rosettes in the adhesive. (See page 19 as needed.)

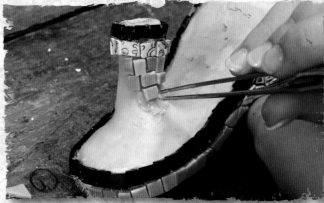

13. FILL IN REST OF INSTEP

Fill in the area of the instep around the rosettes with small pieces of tile.

14. TILE HEEL

Tile the heel using the pattern used on top of the shoe. Wrap a row of very small squares around the edge of the heel. Then wrap a row of pieces cut from the plate. Fill in the rest of the heel with additional very small squares.

15. TILE BOTTOM OF SHOE AND GROUT

Tile the bottom of the shoe in one color using randomly cut pieces. These pieces can be larger than the rest of the pieces used on the shoe since the bottom is relatively flat and also because it won't be seen when the shoe is on display. When you are finished, grout the shoe, if desired. (See Grouting on page 16 as needed.)

Sculpting Epoxy to Transform Objects

With the help of sculpting epoxy (like Magic Sculp) you can transform just about any soft or flexible object into a piece of mosaic art. You can also add fun embellishments like the wings on the shoe below. In addition to leather shoes, try tiling a ballet slipper or a hat.

Even pillows can be sculpted! Nope, a real pillow is not actually used— the mosaic is built around wire mesh, but that is a whole other book!

SLIPPER EMPORIUM

Below is a table housing just a few of the many shoes I have tiled over the years, including a ballet slipper in progress and beautiful winged high heel. Below the table is a mosaic pillow.

At Home

Bathing in the Beauty

I live with my mosaics, and I bathe in their beauty—sometimes literally. I took a boring blue and white bathroom with a linoleum floor and plain tub and made it into what I think is mosaic heaven. For the lower walls of the room, I used stucco and then applied a wash using several layers of gold and bronze metallic glazes. The upper walls and ceiling are mosaicked with large patterned Mexican and Italian ceramic tiles, cut into smaller shapes with my wet saw and a tile nipper. The floor and the bathtub are both made of glass tiles. The bottom of the tub and parts of the floor are created in the reverse (or indirect) method, where the tiles are set upside-down onto a sticky adhesive tape and then flipped into the glue on the surface of the substrate. This ensures a flawlessly smooth finish once the tiles are set. The rest of the bathtub is done directly (setting tiles directly onto the tub). I set plants and flowers around the large mirror, which reflects the mosaic beauty of the walls, turning a very small bathroom into a room that feels opulent and spacious.

(Left) The bathroom in my home.

Teschi Skull

I began creating skulls as a way to connect to the Mexican celebration of Day of the Dead, during which altars of keepsakes would not be complete without a decorated skull. This skull, which I named *The Blushing Bride*, is based on the story of Marianne Primack (whom you can read about on 58). This project is not for the mosaic faint-hearted.; it requires many cuts and small pieces. Plus, there are very few flat areas—it's all curves, indentations and undulations. Often I have to search craft and thrift stores for the right embellishments. So if nothing else, let this skull be an inspiration. But if you embark on this project, gather your materials from everywhere and anywhere and let the fun begin!

WHAT YOU'LL NEED:

Tesserae (see page 18)

cut tiles: large rectangles (2 colors), rectangles of varying heights (red), very small squares (1 color), small pieces (pale pink, red and white)

millefiori (about 2 oz. of one pattern, whole slices and half-cuts)

large gem

rhinestone chain

5 or 6 found jewelry pieces

Tools and Materials

wheeled glass cutters and/or tile nippers

styrofoam skull

tile primer

paintbrush

permanent pen

silicone adhesive

long tweezers

Grouting Kit (p. 16)

three porcelain flowers

1. DIVIDE SKULL AND SET FOCAL POINT

Prime the skull (see Priming on page 15), but only seal the skull (do not sand or score). Then divide the skull into sections using a permanent pen. Set the focal point on the center of the forehead using silicone adhesive. You can use a cabochon as I did or use any large gem. Add small rectangles around the focal point and top those with very small squares.

2. PLACE MILLEFIORI ALONG SECTION LINES

Fill in the bottom of the focal point with a row of about eight millefiori. Then add thin lines of silicone adhesive over your pen lines and place millefiori along all the lines. Also, add millefiori to frame the ear sockets.

3. FRAME EYE SOCKETS IN WHITE

Outline the eye sockets with white squares. You may need to snip off the corners of a few squares to better follow the curves of the socket. Be patient during this process! Cutting tiles to fit and working pieces tightly often requires lots of snipping to get the angles right. Repeat to frame the nose socket.

4. FILL IN LIPS

Draw the shape of the lips first, then fill in with red tile pieces. You'll need two angular shapes for the top of the lips, and rectangles of varying heights for the rest of the lips. Place the larger pieces toward the center and the smaller ones near the edges, filling in the shape of her seductive lips.

Digging up a Skull

Where in the world do you find a skull? First off, no, I do not use real skulls. Not that you couldn't, but I'm sure there are laws about that sort of thing. If you plan to unearth ancient burial sites, please check city ordinances.

There are a number of places online to find skulls. Generally, when skulls are sold in stores, they are sold as seasonal items around Halloween, so keep your eyes open around that ghoulish time of year and check local stores. Skulls can be made from several different materials, but the ones I prefer are made from styrofoam, which allows you to shave off a little here and there to adjust for easier tiling. It's a lot cheaper than plastic surgery!

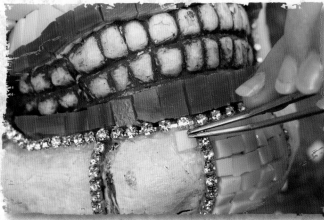

5. MAKE CHEEKS BLUSH
Set small pink pieces to give blush to the cheeks. You may need to cut pieces smaller to hug the curves. Fill in any remaining space on the face above the teeth with pieces of white tile. Then adhere a small piece of costume jewelry on the bridge of the nose, between the eyes.

6. ATTACH RHINESTONE CHAIN TO JAW
Draw lines around the bottom jaw, creating sections. Attach pieces of rhinestone chain along the lines. Also attach a longer piece of chain all along the jawline (right below the lips). Fill in the sections with white tiles cut into very small squares.

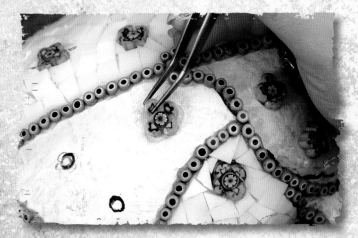

7. SET ROSETTES INTO TOP SECTIONS
Work on the sections at the top of the skull (including sections surrounding the focal point from step 1). In each of the sections, set 2 or 3 millefiori rosettes (see page 19 as needed).

8. FILL IN SECTIONS
Fill in the area around the rosettes with randomly cut pieces of white tile. Remember, working over curved surfaces requires smaller cuts, so cut pieces as needed to follow the curves.

9. ADD JEWELRY TO BACK OF SKULL

Set pieces of costume jewelry into the sections at the back of the skull. Add a single millefiori to accent the bottom of the jewelry. Then fill in the sections with more small tile pieces. Also fill in with randomly cut pieces any remaining parts of the skull that have not been tiled.

10. GROUT AND ATTACH FLOWERS

Once the silicone dries and tiles are stable, grout the skull. (See page 17 as needed.) Then place ceramic flowers in the eyes and nose sockets. Apply generous amounts of silicone adhesive to the backs of the flowers in areas where the petals will touch the skull. Then place the flowers and allow the adhesive to dry.

CARMEN MIRANDA SKULL

Carmen Miranda was always an inspiration to me, breathing her exotic and flamboyant energy into the dramatic life I was seeking as I grew up just a stone's throw away from Hollywood. This skull, I hope, captures the same colorful zaniness that Carmen intoxicated her audiences with.

Vetro Frantumato
Crash Glass Collage

Creating mosaics using tempered (crash) glass is magical. In fact, I call it good-tempered glass. Take flat images pieced into a collage and set them under sections of shattered glass and you'll see a transformation take place. The mundane becomes the sacred. Ordinary becomes iconoclastic. What is it about looking deep within and discovering what lies below that's so intense? That's what's magical. For this project, we'll layer paper, photos, glitter, gold leaf and iridescent cellophane under tempered and plate glass to create a distinctive and innovative mosaic piece. This medium always makes people ask, "How did you do that?" Find out now!

Honorable Mention: Two great pioneers of this method are Mo Ringey (aka "the fridge queen") and Ellen Blakeley.

WHAT YOU'LL NEED:

Tesserae (see page 18)

cut tiles: small rectangles (1 color)

tesserae to fill in as needed (tiles, millefiori, rhinestones, flat-backed marbles, etc.)

Tools and Materials

wheeled glass cutters and/or tile nippers

plywood board

tempered glass (¼" [6mm] thick)

plastic sheeting

hammer

patterned paper (2 sheets)

scissors

two-part water-soluble liquid epoxy

paintbrush

paper with Chinese writing

red and gold acrylic paint

sponge

plate glass (¼" [6mm] thick)

permanent pen

pistol grip

running pliers

large vintage image

small vintage images

craft stick

glitter

gold leaf

tweezers

iridescent cellophane

Grouting Kit (p. 16)

1. CHECK AND CLEAN GLASS

Check that your glass sheet is truly tempered glass. If it is, you'll see the etched insignia in the corner of the glass sheet. Clean both sides of the tempered glass before shattering it.

2. BREAK GLASS

Wrap the glass sheet in plastic and hit it with a hammer in one sharp blow to the outside corner. (If you hit the glass in the middle, it will shatter differently, often making sharp pieces that are difficult to work with.) If the glass doesn't shatter, wedge a screwdriver under it and hit it again on the edge.

3. LET GLASS CRACK

The glass, once hit, will expand and the plastic will help keep it contained. The crackling will continue for a couple of minutes after impact. (I find this sound delightful.)

Choosing Your Glass

Any glass or window supplier can make a piece of tempered glass to order. As far as thickness, I don't recommend a sheet thinner than ¼" (6mm), as thinner glass will fracture more, which creates tighter crack lines that are difficult to see through. When choosing plate glass to cover images used within your mosaic, be sure to use pieces the same thickness as your tempered glass.

Epoxy versus Epoxy

When it comes to Magic Smooth Epoxy versus Douglas and Sturgess, it can be a great debate: Both are water soluble and nontoxic, and both dry translucent to transparent and have a one-hour working time. The good news is, you don't have to choose. Both work well for this project, but you should keep in mind how you will use the epoxy before you pick some to try. Here's a rundown.

Magic Smooth
Magic Smooth, a two-part epoxy, has a thicker viscosity and stays put. I use it mostly to attach background paper to wood (or other background surfaces) and all subsequent layers of paper, fabric, borders and images. This can also be used with metal.

Douglas and Sturgess
Douglas and Sturgess also has a two-part epoxy (hardener #8140 and resin # 7828), but it is thinner, more viscous and moves more like liquid. Since it moves and flows so freely and dires clear, this is an excellent choice for spreading over an entire finished collage (prior to setting the glass).

Why not silicone?
When laying in the pieces of glass (see next page), it helps to have a lot of flexibility and slide room to push your pieces around to fit. Silicone grabs too quickly and doesn't slide as well.

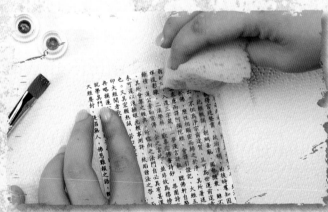

4. CUT AND ADHERE PATTERNED PAPER
Cut a sheet of patterned paper (or gift wrap) to the size of your board. Spread a thin layer of epoxy adhesive (I used Magic Smooth) across the board and adhere the paper to it, smoothing out any wrinkles. Cut four 1" x 9" (3cm x 20cm) strips and add adhesive (either the epoxy or a glue stick) to the backs. Attach them to the edges of the board, smoothing as needed.

5. CUT AND PAINT PAPER WITH WRITING
Cut out the large vintage image and place it over the paper with Chinese writing to determine its size (the paper should allow for about a 1" [3cm] border around the image). Cut the paper. Then brush a mix of red and gold acrylic paint over the paper, then dab the paint with a damp sponge to create a mottled, aged look. Once it dries, adhere the paper to the center of the board.

6. CUT PLATE GLASS FOR VINTAGE PHOTOS

Lay pieces of plate glass over the small vintage photos and cut them to fit. (If you have circular images, use square pieces of glass.) With a permanent pen, mark the glass where you need to cut, then cut. (See Cutting Stained Glass on page 23.) Remove all pen marks from glass and set it aside.

7. ADHERE VINTAGE PHOTOS TO BOARD

Adhere your vintage photos to the board. Set the largest one in the center of the Chinese writing paper and scatter the others around. Use the epoxy to adhere the images.

8. ATTACH PLATE GLASS OVER PHOTOS

Using the edge of a craft stick, spread an even layer of liquid epoxy (I used Douglas and Sturgess) over the surface of the board. Then place your plate glass pieces (from step 6) over their corresponding images. When adding the large, middle piece of glass, add a glob of epoxy to the center of it first and then press it into the epoxy on the board. Remove any excess epoxy that seeps out under the edges using the craft stick.

9. SET PLATE GLASS AND TILE ALONG BORDER

Place your border pieces along the edges of the board, alternating the plate glass with rectangles of tile. It's not neccessary to add epoxy to the glass pieces before adhering them because small pieces are not as susceptible to air bubbles as larger pieces are.

10. ADD GLITTER AND GOLD LEAF

Sprinkle glitter around the center image to form an irregular border. (Neatness doesn't count!) Add additional glitter in spots around the board as well. Also add flecks of gold leaf, using the tweezers, in spots around the board.

11. ADD PIECES OF CELLOPHANE

Tear pieces of iridescent cellophane and place those around the board for additional shimmer. Then add a bit of epoxy over the cellophane so the tempered glass will stick. If you added a thick layer of glitter and/or gold leaf (in step 10) add a bit of epoxy over those areas as well.

12. AFFIX TEMPERED GLASS ISLANDS

Fill in the remaining spaces on the board with the tempered glass. Start by setting larger pieces, called islands. You can break the islands into smaller pieces, to create more lines for grouting, after you've set them in the epoxy. Press down firmly on either side of a crack and gently pull the island of glass apart. Fill in around the islands with smaller sections and single pieces of glass (called shake).

13. FILL REMAINING SPACES

Fill in any odd remaining spaces with pieces of tile or glass. You can also fill in spaces with millefiori, small flat-backed marbles, gems or rhinestones. Watch how you embedd the tesserae in the adhesive. You want an even height among the tesserae and the glass pieces. Allow the collage to set for twenty-four hours before grouting.

14. PREPARE GROUT

Make a looser, runnier mixture of grout than typical (so as not to dislodge any tiny pieces). The consistency should be similar to cake batter.

15. GROUT THE PIECE

Spread grout over the whole piece, being careful to fill in all the tiny crevices. (See page 17 as needed.)

La Danse

LA DANSE

This crash glass piece was worked inside a picture frame, over the glass. This work is unintentionally multicultural: The background is script from a Chinese book, lightly painted over in golden yellow. The ballerina is photo taken from a Russian opera. The Eiffel Tower rises above her, creating a harmony between all of the images. My daughter, Kiah created this piece.

Chapter
4

Art Gallery

INSPIRING MOSAICS FROM ARTISTS AROUND THE WORLD

Enter into the gallery of free-thinking artists, now bound together in this book, revealing the not-so-secret society of mosaicists. Whether their purpose is to inspire others' creation, adorn walls or just sit as an expression of the artists themselves, these pieces are each a gift to behold. They speak of color, movement, detail and the divine. And the thread that connects them all is millefiori.

In this chapter you will see a wide variety of ways in which millefiori can be set and manipulated to produce a unique effect. Millefiori may be used as slices or not cut at all. Some artists may use only one or two millefiori in their entire piece, or they may cluster pieces together in colonies.

Here is the gallery of wonderful art for your delight and inspiration ... .

Christmas Pheasant

Martin Cheek

Broadstairs, Kent, United Kingdom

Dreams of India

Laurie Mika

Encinitas, California

Chador

Dusciana Bravura

Ravenna, Italy

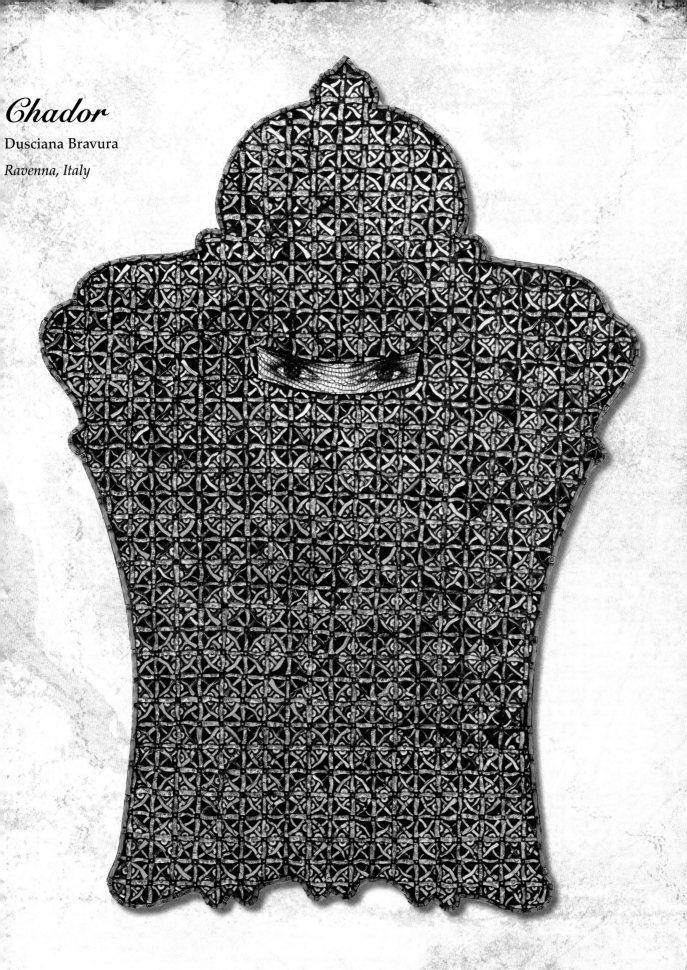

Valentina Through the Looking Glass

Arlene Piarulli

Crema, Italy

Ladies of Venice

Susan Gardner

Brooklyn, New York

Sunshine Girl / If Chairs Had Hands

Diann Bartnick

Grand Rapids, Michigan

Pounce

Christine Brallier

Goleta, California

She's Green With Envy

Kathy R. Brogden

Birmingham, Alabama

Byzantine Cross

Shannon Frischknecht

Arcata, California

Surreptitious Dialogue

Lilian Broca

Vancouver, British Columbia, Canada

Forbidden Fruit

Marian Shapiro

Bayview, New South Wales, Australia

Ladybug
Faducci

North San Juan, California

Fox Hunt
Jackie Stack Lagakos

Lindenwold, New Jersey

Let the Party Begin

Robin Friedman

Bayside, California

Untitled

Virginia Gardner

Earlysville, Virginia

Keep Me Warm

Julie Dilling

Plano, Texas

Sputnik 3D

Lynne Chinn

Plano, Texas

Six Virgins

Marilyn Abrams

Glen Cove, New York

The Four Seasons

Laurie Mika

Encinitas, California

Texture Evolution

Yulia Hanansen

Ann Arbor, Michigan

New Orleans Lady

Gila Rayberg

Pensacola, Florida

Nashville

Leslie Roberts

Murfeesburo, Tennessee

Grace Received

Patricia Ormsby

Toronto, Ontario, Canada

Muse #2

Karen Pearle

Oakland, California

Bird of Stars

Kate Rattray

Wells, Somerset, United Kingdom

L'Ambasciatrice

Julie Richey

Irving, Texas

Twister

Yulia Hanansen

Ann Arbor, Michigan

Yellow Martian

Kathy R. Brogden

Birmingham, Alabama

Tree of Life

Irina Charny

Irvine, California

Greek Woman

Nancy Shelby

Redway, California

Turquoise and Millefiori Skull

Crystal Thomas

Woodinville, Washington

Spatola
Dusciana Bravura

Ravenna, Italy

Golden Pheasant
Martin Cheek

Broadstairs, Kent, United Kingdom

Dragon in Dreamtime

Charlotte Cornish

Abottskerswell, Devon, United Kingdom

Mr. Froggy

Suzan Germond

Austin, Texas

Dreamer

Carole Choucair Oueijan

Hacienda Heights, California

Pink Wildflowers

Laura Rendlen

Glen Ellyn, Illinois

Summer Forest

Virginia Gardner

Earlysville, Virginia

Crazy Clouds Mirror

Vaishali Sanghavi

Los Altos, California

Bird in Hand

Cassie Edmonds

Tyler, Texas

Index

Resources

Adhesives

MAPEI
www.mapei.us

MAC Craft Glue
www.macglue.net

Magic Sculp
www.magicsculp.com

Douglas and Sturgess
www.artstuf.com

Mastic Pigment

Diamond Tech
www.diamondtechglass.com

Tiles & Tools
www.tilesandtools.eu

Smalti

Mosaic Smalti
www.mosaicsmalti.com

di Mosaico
www.dimosaico.com

Smalti
www.smalti.com

Millefiori

Murano Millefiori
www.muranomillefiori.com

Xinamarie Mosaici
www.xinamarie.com

Annafietta
www.annafietta.it.

Who Is Laurel Skye?

As her daughter Kiah describes Laurel, "She is middle-aged, which means she's been around for a pretty long time. Once skinny and called 'chicken legs' she now lives in her stretch jeans, much of her body scarred from a house fire. She is a cancer and head-trauma survivor. Four children, and one passed on. She is quick to expound on all things mosaic, which is her passion. She is a clutter freak. Laurel has creaky joints and is not formally educated. She is more clever than smart, more resourceful than clever, and always grateful to wake up in the morning and pull on her Uggs."

Kiah goes on, "Take antique lamps and ornately carved cabinets, hundreds of Middle Eastern and African woven rugs, an Egyptian sarcophagus, rooms full of miniature leather camels and Tibetan masks, glass pieces as brilliant as fire itself, a love for fashion and artistic extremes, and you have Laurel Skye. Not exactly a housewife from Wisteria Lane, she can be found in this fantastical world she has created for herself. Once we know how to access a world such as this, something changes in our biorhythms, something that tells us what we are taking in; it's odd and wacky, magical, and it's a wonder to behold. That is Laurel Skye. Her art, her mosaics, are a reflection of all of this."

From skulls, mirrors, shoes, toasters, crutches and musical instruments covered with tesserae Laurel has been creating mosaics for twelve years, along with her daughter, in her home in Arcata, California. She lives with Kiah, her bouncing sheepdog Dharma, Dolma and Dorje (her Himalayan cats), and her imaginary boyfriend, Tao Tsing, who all help to keep her sane.

You can visit Laurel over at her Web site: http://web.me.com/laurelskye.

Find more inspiration in these other North Light Books.

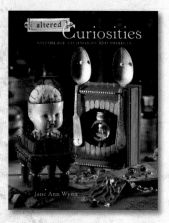

Altered Curiosities

Jane Ann Wynn

Discover a curious world of assemblage with projects that have a story to tell! As author Jane Ann Wynn shares her unique approach to mixed-media art, you'll learn to alter, age and transform odd objects into novel new works of your own creation. Step-by-step instructions guide you in making delightfully different projects that go way beyond art for the wall.
ISBN-10: 1-58180-972-7; ISBN-13: 978-1-58180-972-5; paperback, 128 pages, Z0758

Tiles Gone Wild

Chrissie Grace

Chrissie Grace, author of the best-selling *Wild Tiles*, will send your mosaic work in new directions with *Tiles Gone Wild*. You'll learn how to combine traditional, commercial tile with handmade clay tiles, crushed glass, stained glass and mixed-media elements in twenty whimsical step-by-step projects.
ISBN 10: 1-60061-081-1; ISBN 13: 978-1-60061-081-3; paperback, 128 pages, Z1929

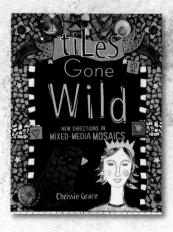

Secrets of Rusty Things

Michael de Meng

Learn how to transform common, discarded materials into shrine-like assemblages infused with personal meaning and inspired by ancient myths and metaphors. As you follow along with author Michael de Meng, you'll see the magic in creating art using unlikely objects such as rusty doorpulls, old sardine tins and other quirky odds and ends. ISBN 10: 1-58180-928-X; ISBN 13: 978-1-58180-928-2; paperback, 128 pages, Z0556

Mixed Media Mosaics

Laurie Mika

Learn to craft highly textural and vividly colored icons, boxes, tables, items of personal adornment and more using a combination of manufactured and handmade tiles. Step-by-step demos will teach you to make your own polymer clay tiles using techniques such as painting and glazing, stamping and mixing pigments and powders with clay. Also included are ideas and techniques helpful for personalizing your artwork.
ISBN-10: 1-58180-983-2; ISBN-13: 978-1-58180-983-1; paperback, 128 pgs, Z0823

These and other fine North Light Books are available at your local craft retailer, bookstore or online supplier, or visit our Web site at www.mycraftivitystore.com.